STANDARD LOAN

UNLESS RECALLED BY ANOTHER READER
THIS ITEM MAY BE BORROWED FOR

FOUR WEEKS

To renew, telephone:
01243 816089 (Bishop Otter)
01243 816099 (Bognor Regis)

Line drawings by Heather Hacking

First Published in 1994 by
BELAIR PUBLICATIONS LIMITED
P.O. Box 12, Twickenham, TW1 2QL, England

©1994 Stephanie Mudd and Hilary Mason

Series Editor Robyn Gordon
Designed by Richard Souper
Photography by Kelvin Freeman
Typesetting by Belair
Printed and Bound in Hong Kong by World Print Ltd
ISBN 0 947882 27 8

Acknowledgements

The authors and publishers would like to thank: Tina Etheridge, Maureen Manuel, Cathy Whalen, staff and pupils of Mousehold First School, Norwich; Jaqui Moss, staff and pupils of John of Gaunt First School, Aylsham; Ruth Flint, staff and pupils of Runcton Holme C.E.V.A. School, Kings Lynn, Norfolk, for their invaluable contributions in the preparation of classroom displays.

The authors would also like to say thank you to the children of their local Saturday group for all their contributions and enthusiasm.

Contents

Introduction

In a Moment provides class, substitute and supply teachers with an instant bank of short-term topic activities. There are many occasions during a school year when you may need mini-topics ready to start at a moment's notice. You will find them particularly useful for supply cover; making a quick revisit to a topic area; at the beginning of a new term, or for following up an outside visit.

The book has been planned so that you can start topics 'in a moment'. The activities can all be done in and around the school, generally using only those materials which come readily to hand. There are no long-term growth or diary-type projects and it will not be necessary to organise trips out. The aim is to get the children involved straight away - without having to rely on information or resources gathered from outside school.

Grouped under **Collections** (page 50) there are five more topics for which you will need some simple, easily found outside resources. There are suggestions for recycling your old cards and buttons into new classroom activities, ideas for autumn seeds and leaves, snails, and flowers.

Five of the topics are based on popular story books, available in libraries, bookshops and school book corners (see **Starting with a Book,** page 60). Begin these topics by reading the book with the children, giving them time to discuss the story line, characters and illustrations, as appropriate.

You know best how you like to organise your teaching groups. Many of the activities allow for all the children to be involved with the same task at the same time, or you may choose to have several activities running alongside each other. Select from the range of suggestions to suit the age and ability of the children.

Arranged under subject headings for instant accessibility, the topics are based on the National Curriculum Programmes of Study. The headings we have used are: English, maths, science, technology, art and craft, humanities, music and hall time. At the beginning of each topic, the 'Starters' give you a few ideas for helping the children to focus on the themes you are introducing.

A list (on page 7l) recommends stories, poems, or songs relating to the themes. Further general references for story, poetry and music anthologies are given under 'Resources' (page 7l).

The 'five minute fillers' (page 70) are ideas for carpet activities and games to help you make best use of those 'spare moments' that arise in any school day.

Stephanie Mudd and Hilary Mason

Pleased to meet you

Set up an easy rapport between you and the children with some of these 'register time' activites. Try them as a new start to term, during emergency cover, and on supply teaching days.

Getting to know the children
● Call out a name - ask the next child on the register to tell you one nice thing about the previous person.
● As they answer their names in registration, ask the children to tell you one thing about themselves (age, favourite food or colour, brothers/sisters).
● Call out names: individuals respond and introduce a friend, e.g. 'I am Sanjit. This is Jamie'.
● Try calling out names and responses in a range of different voices: quietly/loudly, happy/sad mood; in the manner of a story character...
● Say and clap (or sing) the rhythm of individual names, and ask children to echo them.
● Ask each of the children to say their name and this time add a describing word beginning with the same initial sound, e.g. Super Sally, Daring Dario.
● Play 'Guess Who?' Describe individual children (clothes, actions etc.) - can the children name the mystery classmate?
● Appeal for the children's help to distinguish between class members with the same name. Consider how, for example, the two Hannahs are the same and different (hair, eye colour, clothes...).

Getting to know you
● What can the children deduce from the clues in your bag? (See display photograph.) Do you enjoy sport, have a car, sometimes travel to other parts of the country/world, love music? Where might you be going after school?
● Share your initial impressions of the school/class with the children. What else can they tell you about: the size/type of school; the models or topic display you admired as you came in.
● Describe significant aspects of your journey to school: landmarks, major roads; how long it took; type of transport. Can the children work out if you live nearby or further away?
● By asking questions and listening to your responses, what can the children find out about you in two minutes?

Alphabet

Starters

Sensitise the children to different sorts of print, letter shape and size in books, lists and on display boards, posters etc. Play games like 'I Spy' and 'I packed my bag' to reinforce letter/sound recognition. Look at a book index and talk about alphabetical order.

English

- Make your own alphabet strip showing upper and lower case for each letter. Use different typefaces cut out from magazines, newspapers and catalogues.
- Take a letter of the alphabet and brainstorm as many things as you can think of beginning with that initial sound. How many can the children include in a composite picture? (See display photograph.)
- Make up short, alliterative sentences and illustrate them (see display photograph).
- How can the alphabet help us to organise things in school (register, address lists etc.)? Try putting computer disks, children's folders, job lists into alphabetical order.
- How many animals/objects can you find in a dictionary beginning with a chosen letter?
- Can the children write without using the alphabet? Try a message to a friend using pictures only.

- **Explore the kinds of scripts** available on computer (size, print/cursive/gothic, italics, etc.). Print some out and use the letters to make your own 'QWERTY' keyboard plan.

Maths

- Use link bricks to make your initials/name. Which letter covers the most space? Will any of the letters tessellate?
- Predict, then chart, the most common letter in the children's names, or in a small sample of text.
- Count and chart the number of letters in your name. Who has the longest/shortest name? Try showing comparisons using cube trays, threading beads, writing on squared paper.
- Can you make letter shapes on a calculator by keying in figures and turning the display upside down? Explore the numbers pressed to give words such as: oil, bell, ill, lose.

- **Find out which letters have a line of symmetry** - can the children draw them in?

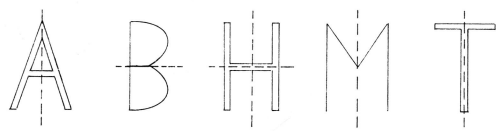

Humanities

- Make an alphabetical list of towns/countries the children have visited; or, a street directory of children's addresses.
- Look at letters used in road/information signs and map symbols. Design some letter signs to mark up the school office, library, hall...avoid getting *cook* and *caretaker* signs confused!
- Make up a mnemonic to help remember compass directions NSEW, e.g. Never Eat Soggy Waffles.
- Choose an initial letter and use maps or index to find three local street names, or towns/rivers, beginning with that letter.

Art and Craft/Design and Technology

- Make personalised wrapping paper by printing a letter in a regular pattern. Use old Plasticine, press print, or raised card to make the printing block.
- Look at different typefaces and alphabetical scripts. Try writing your name in the same style, e.g. italics, bubble lettering.

● **What do letter shapes suggest to the children (birds, buildings)? Make pictures using letters as a starting point.**

● Make your own stand-up name/initials from junk box materials.
● Make some alphabet dominoes matching pictures with initial letters.

Music
● Try singing the alphabet to help remember the sequence of letters. Can you fit it to a favourite nursery rhyme or song, e.g. Twinkle, twinkle; Humpty Dumpty?
● Explore which letters make long, sustained sounds (ee, oo, mm), or shorter sounds (b, t, c). Take turns to say a letter sound around a circle. The next person says the letter when the previous sound can no longer be heard. Which letters get around the circle quickest?

Hall time
● Shape up! In groups of three, children can try making the shapes of letters with their bodies on the floor. Compare the attempts of different groups - were any letters impossible?
● Creeping letters: children move forwards one pace towards a home base if you call out a letter which is in their initials/first name - who creeps home first?

Boxes and Bottles

Starters
Discuss what boxes/bottles are for (storage, safety, decoration). Look at a range of sizes, shapes, colours and materials - establish what is the same/different about them.

English
● Make a label for a bottle of magic potion. Show the dosage and its magical effects: one teaspoon of tomato sauce, two tablespoons of washing-up liquid...transforms dirty plates into pizzas!
● **Make a story-box mobile.** Write (or draw and caption) a four-frame sequence on a strip of paper folded into four sections. Make into a box shape and hang up.

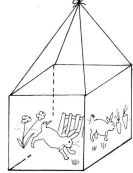

● Place an object inside a box. Write three clues for others to guess what is inside.
● Brainstorm some 'special purpose' boxes, e.g. jewellery box, post box, lunch box. Draw/write what is special about them (see display photograph). You could compile individual contributions into an alphabetical book of boxes.

Maths
● Open out a box and draw the plane shapes you can see. Fold it together again. Can you make a similar box from construction toys?
● Estimate, then count, the number of cubes that will fill a chosen box. Use the same box and try again with other contents (counters, cotton reels, conkers).
● Use a Carroll diagram to sort containers according to characteristics such as: lids/no lids; contents (edible/not); labels/no labels.
● Investigate whether all boxes have the same number of edges, faces, and corners.
● **Estimate, then measure, the tallest/shortest tower** you can make with three boxes.

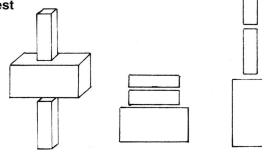

● Make a Plasticine box/bottle. Predict, then draw, which shape you will find as you cut the box in two at different angles.
● What is the greatest/smallest area you can cover with four boxes?

Science/Technology
● Make a lid for a box. Will it slide, have a hinge, or be close fitting?

● **Use junk boxes to make hand puppets** (animals, story characters) and use in role play.

- Investigate how bottles float/sink. What happens when the caps are on/off; a screw-top bottle is filled with water; you punch holes in the side of the bottle?
- Sort containers by the materials from which they are made. Are there any links between the contents/purpose and materials?
- Use bottles/boxes to make a game of quoits. Cut out card rings just the right size to fit over the containers. How can you keep them steady?

Humanities
- What clues can you spot to help you deduce what a junk box/bottle may once have contained? Has it got a label? What shape/size is it? Are there any sediments/smells?
- Use 'sell-by' dates to order your boxes and bottles into a time-line.
- Draw/caption five things you would include in a 'my memories box', e.g. birthday card, teddy, shoe...
- Place two boxes beside, or on top of each other. Draw a side and/or a top view. See if others can match the plans to the boxes.
- How many place names can you find on boxes/bottles? Try sorting into Great Britain/elsewhere.

Music
- How many different ways can you 'play' an empty box? Try fingers and hands (bang, scrape, tap, flick). Explore sounds made with different beaters: ruler, pencil, straw, rolled paper tubes, twig.
- To the rhythm and tune of 'Ten Green Bottles', find different ways of 'playing bottles': blow across; hum into; fill with differing levels of water and use as a xylophone.

Hall time
- Target practice: throw a beanbag into a box or basket; roll balls at bottles/skittles.
- Play 'broken bottles'. Children stand in a circle with the teacher in the centre. Throw a ball to children in turn. Each missed catch carries a forfeit. First go down on one knee; then two knees; one hand behind their backs. Reverse the process for successful catches.

Changes

Starters

Talk about changes you have made so far today, e.g. from sleeping to waking; night to day clothes; changing direction on the journey to school. Show the children how we can change our expressions and voices, and invite them to try it for themselves. Brainstorm more changes.

English

● Use your brainstorm as the basis for a 'changes' class poem (see display photograph).
● Think about times when you change your clothes, e.g. from day to night clothes; outdoor to indoor; P.E., swimming. Make a picture/caption sequence of either getting dressed or undressed.
● Use the dressing-up box (or the imagination) to show how you would change your appearance for a fancy dress party. Draw and label the changes you have made.
● **Show how a simple letter string can be changed into words** by adding letters before and after, e.g. sh + op = shop (shell, ship); an + t = ant; f + an = fan; h+ an + d = hand.

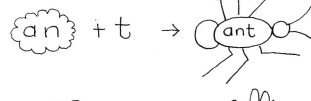

 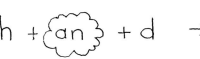

● Recall changes featured in stories and rhymes: the Ugly Duckling changed into a swan; Red Riding Hood's wolf disguised itself; Pinocchio's nose grew. Draw and caption some of these. You could compile them into a class book of 'Story Changes'.

Maths

● **Use four geo-strips to make a square.** Draw the different shapes you can push it into.

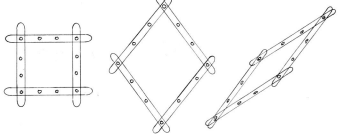

● Draw a simple closed shape. Explore how the shape changes as you move a mirror on the drawing.
● Logi-block changes: in pairs, children take turns to lay down a block which is one attribute different from the one before.
● Change the size of a piece of paper by repeatedly folding it in half. Record the sequence of changes in size by drawing round each new shape you have made.
● Enter the number 8 into a calculator. Keep adding l0. Record the number changes shown on the display.
● Exchange a l0p coin for pennies (or for 2/4/5 coins). Try starting with other coin values.

Science/Technology

● Investigate the different ways of changing the shape of a piece of fabric: scrunch, fold, roll, cut, stretch. Can you do the same with Plasticine, or newspaper?

● **Make a 'changing clown' kit.**
Draw a face shape. Cut out features to place on it: circle/crossed eyes, happy/sad mouth, spiky/curly hair. Now change the clown's appearance.

CHANGES

An egg pops
A caterpillar crawls
A chrysalis changes into a
beautiful butterfly.

Suck an ice lolly
Chilly water glugs down your throat
Making your tongue bright orange.

In olden days, no cars
Just a horse and cart.

Winter - black, bumpy clouds
Grey, grumpy clouds.
Summer - white lumpy clouds
Full of pictures.

Feeling sad
Then happy again.

Growing older and bigger
Growing older and older
Going crinkly.

● How does your reflection change when you look in: back or front of spoons; silver paper; glass bottle; a tin; a bowl of water. Draw what you see.
● Make something to change your appearance, e.g. a false nose, beard, wig or spectacles.

Humanities

● What changes do you have to make to the clothes you wear when the weather changes? Draw/cut out sets of clothes you might wear outside on a rainy, hot, or snowy day.
● How have you changed since you were a toddler? Draw/label three things you can do now that you could not manage then, e.g. reach light switches; use a skipping rope; build with Lego.
● How does the view change when you turn round? Sit in a chair - look straight ahead and list what you see. Make one quarter, half, complete turns - what do you see now?
● Fill a suggestion box with the changes you would like to see in the classroom. Consider: are some areas too noisy? Can you reach the sink? Would you like more cushions?

Music

● Change the tempo: make some body sounds for the children to watch carefully and follow (knee pats, claps, palm rubs). Practise slowing down/speeding up, helping the children to keep pace with you.
● Use voice sounds (oo, ee) to practise changing from loud to soft, high to low, long to short sounds. Introduce hand signals to 'conduct' the changes.

Hall time

● All change: children move around the hall in one direction until they hear you bang the tambourine. This is the signal to change direction. Use the same approach to practise changes of speed and types of movement (hop, skip, wriggle on tummies, etc.).
● Amoebas: keep changing from one shape to another, while keeping your backs (hands/feet) on the floor.

Colour

Starters

Help the children to name and talk about the colours used in their clothes and objects around the room. Which are single/multi-coloured? Brainstorm naming words containing colours, e.g. Ms. Green, goldfish, blackbird, bluebell.

English

● Make up a colour poem in the shape of a rainbow. Write a line about each colour in turn, e.g. Red as a tomato and my measles spots; Orange as the sunset...
● Describe a friend. Focus on colours - of their hair, eyes, clothing. Can others guess who it is?
● Make four-page concertina Colours book for yourself or a younger child. Find or draw pictures for each chosen colour. Add a caption highlighting the colour words.
● **Make a two-frame camouflage cartoon.** Show in the first frame what you are wearing, and in the second where you are hiding.

Maths

● Make colour sequences and describe to a friend to copy. Try patterns using beads, cube towers, logi blocks.
● Sort classroom objects into colour sets. Use a Venn diagram to show objects with more than one colour.
● Are all eyes blue? Conduct a survey to find out.
● Take a small number of junk boxes and chart the colours used on each box. Interpret your findings - which colour is the most commonly (or never) used, and why?
● Play 'Fill the Board'. Use a cube board (pegs/squared paper) and only three colours. Take turns to place a cube on the board, making sure that no two of the same colour are next to each other.

● **Take eight link bricks (two each of green, blue, yellow, red) and fit them together** to make one large cube with each face showing all four colours.

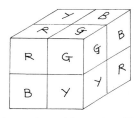

Science/Technology

● Find out what happens to the colour of objects when placed in water. Try a Lego brick, pebble, tissue paper, an old felt-tip pen.

● **Make colour spinners.** Record what happens to the colours as they spin. Try other colour combinations.

● Use junk materials to make a holder to prevent a paint pot toppling over.
● Make a pencil case large enough to hold six crayons.

● **Draw a simple picture outline and devise a key** to show your friend how to colour the picture (initial letter, number, symbol).

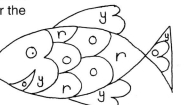

r = red
o = orange
y = yellow

Make still-life drawings, looking carefully at colours

Art and Craft
● Focusing on matching the colours, draw/paint from still life (see display photograph). Compare drawings made from different angles.
● Mix paints by making symmetrical blob prints. Each time, use two primary colours (red, blue or yellow) to make the paint blobs. Observe the colour changes in the patterns.
● Make single-colour collages (fabric, wallpaper, wool, catalogue pictures). Try: woodland (greens); stormy seas (blues); bonfires (red).
● Choose a wax or pencil crayon (chalk, pastel). How many shades can you make by using it different ways - pressing firmly/softly; using it on the tip/side, smudging?
● Make tissue paper patterns using only one colour. Experiment with folded and overlapping paper to achieve different shades.

Music
● Pin up two squares of coloured paper - yellow represents 'softly'; green means 'loudly'. Conduct the children's playing/singing so that they change dynamics as you point first to one colour and then the other. Introduce other colours to represent: dance steps (march, skip, run); moods (angry, surprised); changes of tempo or different instruments (blue means woodblocks play, red is for triangles...)

Hall time
● Play 'Traffic Lights': the children move to the commands: GREEN (run), AMBER (walk), RED (stop).
● Play Colour Tag. Divide the class into four colour groups (use bands). Two children per group are the catchers. The 'its' are only allowed to tag those in their own colour group. On the GO! signal the catchers give chase, linking hands with any team members tagged to form a catch-chain.

Doors and Windows

Starters
Look at the different sorts of doors and windows in the classroom. Discuss their shapes and sizes and why we have them in particular places. How do they open? Identify door furniture: handles, hinges, locks, etc. Brainstorm other types of doors/windows: stable, garage, cat flap, stained glass...

English
● Draw a door shape and add labels - hinge, handle, glass pane, locks, bell, letter box, etc. Do the same for windows.
● Go through the door into a magical land: describe what you find there in five 'senses' lines: 'I see fiery dragons', 'I hear...' etc.
● Compile a doors and windows catalogue for a DIY shop. Include pictures of greenhouse, shed, church, stable, gate. Add captions such as 'This is the supermarket door. It opens automatically.'
● Make a doors and windows Safety Hints poster highlighting, for example, 'Don't lean out'; 'Mind your fingers'.
● Show in a sequence how a window was broken - what led up to the unfortunate incident and what were the consequences?
● Make a collection of class favourite 'knock, knock' jokes.
● **Make some 'guess who?' keyhole cards** (see display photograph). Choose one sort of door to draw. Cut out a keyhole shape and give a clue for what might be seen through the hole - any surprises?

Maths
● Choose two doors (or windows) and compare how they are the same and different: colour, type of handles, opens inwards/outwards.
● Chart which plane shapes you can spot in doors and windows. Have they all got straight edges?
● Survey the position of door handles, knobs, window latches - how many are on the right/left?
● Keep a tally over five minutes of who goes in/out of the classroom door. How many children/adults?

● **How many ways can you arrange 2, 4, 8 panes of equal size** on a l6 square 'window frame'?

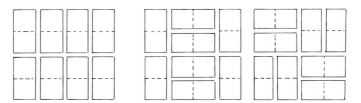

● Find the widest/narrowest door (or window) in class. Remember cupboards and the play house.
● Estimate, then measure, pathways of a door handle, or the bottom of the door. Do the same for windows. Which pathways are curved/straight?

Science/Technology
● Test how well you can hear sounds through doors and windows when they are fully open, closed, ajar.
● Make a check list showing the materials from which doors/windows and their 'accessories' are made.

- Use construction toys to make a building with doors and windows. Make sure they are just the right size and position for a soft toy to go through, and see out, comfortably.
- Think about all the different signs seen on doors: exit, push/pull; do not disturb; open/closed. Try designing one for a school door ('only two in the playhouse'; 'library').
- Make a door/window that opens out and stays fastened securely. Try folding card, paper fasteners, string or tape joiners.

Humanities
- Which visitors to your home might you see as you look out of the window? **Draw a window frame with four panes.** Illustrate and label your visitors, e.g. milkman, meter reader, relatives, friends.

- Draw a simple plan of the classroom showing the position of doors/windows. Try using a simple colour code or symbol to distinguish between doors and windows on your plan.
- Draw the view from a school window and label features such as: hills, shop, mosque, factory, clouds.
- Choose a view from a school window. What do you like/dislike about it? Is it colourful, dull, interesting?

Hall time
- Look through the window: describe to the children what you can see (real or imaginary) through the window. Ask them to represent (in pairs) your description through body shape and movement, e.g. houses with pointed roofs; someone chasing a hat round a windy garden; a melting snowman.

Get the Message

Starters

Discuss the children's ideas about what messages are. Brainstorm the different ways messages are given and received: speaking, telephone, television, radio, posters, body language (see English). Play 'Chinese Whispers' to focus on how messages can sometimes change as they get passed on.

English
- Draw/cut out pictures of different 'message givers'. Write underneath what they are, and the message they give, e.g. 'This is an alarm clock. It rings to wake me up.'
- What sorts of telephone conversations do we have (chatty, enquiries, making appointments)? Role play, or show in speech bubbles, how some of these conversations might go.
- Make up a poem linking a message with a special occasion: 'You're feeling unwell - get better soon'; 'It's Holi - have fun', etc.
- Have a class 'notice board' (use a blackboard or large sheet of paper) for children to leave reminder notes or messages for each other during the day.
- Try writing a message using only pictures and symbols. Can a friend understand it?
- Draw/write step-by-step instructions to show somebody how to make a snack or wash hair.

Maths
- Show on a Venn diagram 'message givers' found in class, in school, and in the home.
- Survey who in the class has a radio, video or computer. How can you best show this information (mapping or Venn diagrams, pictogram or graph)?
- Chart where in school you find messages shown as numbers (rulers, clock, thermometer, tape counter). What do the numbers mean? Which are shown as a straight line or on dials?

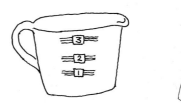

- **Use a jug/bottle to make a capacity measure.** Mark the side showing levels for l, 2, 3, cups full of sand/water.

- Can the children make a class timetable? Show (in picture sequence or chart form) major markers in the day - hall times, lunch, etc.

Science/Technology
- How do facial expressions convey messages? Can you draw your friend's face as: happy, sad, angry, excited?
- What messages do the senses give you? Write a line for each sense: 'My hands tell me the water is cold; my nose tells me the toast is burnt...'
- Try lip reading. Can a partner understand whose name you are saying, or your important message?
- Draw a picture of yourself and plan where you might hide a secret message, e.g. under your collar/hat; down your sock; behind your belt.
- Design a telephone message pad. Allow space for who called, their message, time, date, etc.

Humanities
- Survey languages children know about. Which ones do they speak themselves? Which have they heard at home, on holiday, or on television?
- Spot school 'message givers': signs, labels, clocks, fire alarm, etc. Describe, or plot on a map, where you found them and the message they relay.
- **Make up a picture symbol for a radio, television or book.**

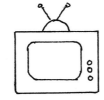 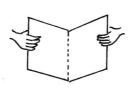 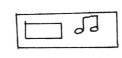

Make a photomontage on how we send and receive messages

● Give clear directions for a friend to take a message to the secretary's office (cook or caretaker).

Music
● Decide, with the children, on hand signals meaning sing/play softly, loudly or stop (e.g. hands placed close together or far apart). Take turns to conduct the group using these signals.
● **Ask the children to draw some picture scores.** How will they show things such as : which instruments to play, which order to play them, or how many beats to play?

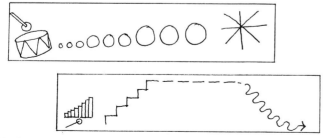

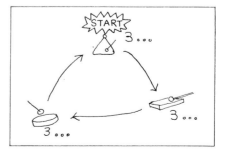

Hall time
● Mime opening a present. Can others guess what is inside? Focus on: facial expression, size of parcel, shape of contents, how you use it.
● Listen and move: try matching movements to tambourine sounds, e.g. tap means walk; shake means skip; bang means freeze...

Hands and Feet

Starters
Play action games involving hands and feet such as Simon Says, and favourite finger rhymes (see Anthologies page 71). What do we wear on our hands and feet (shoes, boots, socks, gloves, jewellery)? Can the children name places within walking distance of home/school? Practise road safety hand signals.

English
● Mime jobs/activities where hands are central: baking, cleaning cars, etc. Can others guess what you are doing?
● Think of five things you have done with your hands today. Write each one of these on fingers of a cut-out hand shape.
● Make a 'Keep your feet fit' poster for a swimming pool, showing one aspect of foot care: 'Dry between your toes'; 'Please use the foot bath'; 'Don't share towels'.
● Talk about what having 'green fingers' means. Make up a story describing what happens when the gardener made plants grow too well. Did they grow feet, reach up to a magical land...?
● Invent foot tongue-twisters using the initial 'f' sound, e.g. 'Frieda's furry feet flip and flop'.

Maths
● Weigh your shoes. Whose are heaviest/lightest? Is the biggest shoe also the heaviest?
● Try picking up a handful of small objects, e.g. cubes, beads, straws. Estimate, count, then record how many you picked up in each try.
● Collect and display data about the children's socks/tights. Who is wearing long/short socks; patterned/plain etc?
● Measure how many hands/feet fit: along a table, blackboard, metre stick, edge of the carpet.
● Estimate, measure and compare how far you and a friend can: roll, kick, throw a ball.

Science
● Take a Plasticine print of a hand or foot. Add card labels identifying the different parts: instep, nails, palms, soles, etc.
● **Survey the types of fastenings used on shoes** (Velcro, buckles, laces). Draw/list under each heading where else these fastenings are used: anoraks, belts, bags.

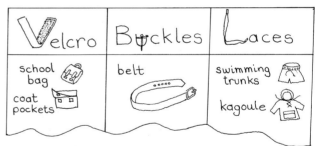

● Investigate the efficiency of different materials for drying hands: towels, paper, tissue, greaseproof paper, plastic.
● Compare how well you can do things with your left and right hands: drawing a face, picking up cubes, threading beads, unscrewing a lid.
● Can you recognise a friend's face through touch alone? Which feature helped you most - hair, glasses, earrings?

Art and Craft/Technology
● **Turn your hand into a bear** (monster, witch). Cut out a hand/paw shape. Make a strap to go across the palm from a strip of paper or card. Embellish with fur, false nails, etc.

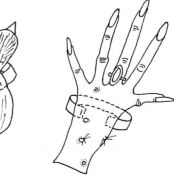

- Make finger-hole puppets (see photographs). The finger holes could become rabbits' ears, a clown's legs...
- Design a carrier bag for a shoe shop. Will it have handles, a shop name or logo? How big does it need to be?
- Paint a patterned sock on one side of a folded piece of paper. Refold to take a blob print and make a pair.
- Use finger painting to illustrate a famous character associated with shoes: Cinderella; The Old Woman who lived in a shoe; the 'fine lady' on her way to Banbury Cross.

Music
- Listen to the sounds your feet make as you march, jump, tip-toe, patter. Try making similar sound patterns on instruments. Put some together as a short sound sequence: walk down the path, run for the bus, stamp when you miss it, jump in a puddle, shuffle home wet.
- All change: establish a steady hand clap pattern. Children join in - ready to change their hand sounds as soon as they spot you changing from claps to taps (flicks, slaps, nail rubs).

Hall time
- Pass a ball without using hands/feet. Try under chins, armpits, crooked elbows, between the knees.
- Move around on different parts of the foot: tip-toes, heels, sides, one heel and one toe.
- Make shapes on the floor using: two hands/one foot; one hand/one foot. Try balancing and travelling like this.

Holes

Starters
Identify and discuss holes on the children themselves: their clothes (arm holes, trouser legs, collars, jewellery...); body holes: mouth, nostrils, ears, etc. Brainstorm other sorts of holes the children know about (see photograph). Play 'holey I-Spy' with objects around the room.

English
- Which letters of the alphabet have holes in them? Try making some from Plasticine, paper, play dough.
- Drawing on your initial brainstorm, make up a 'Holes Everywhere' poem. Begin each line with 'Holes in...'. End each verse with 'Holes, holes everywhere'.
- Make a peep-hole book. Draw pictures of holey household objects (plug hole, colander, mug). Look through the cut-out hole - guess what it is.
- Show in a speech bubble what you might say to explain the hole in your new jeans. This could be 'real' ('I fell off the swing') or fantastic ('A monster nibbled them').
- **Write some clues to describe what holey object may have fallen out of your pocket.** Display like this:

Maths
- How many different holey objects can you thread on a lace in one minute?
- How many 'clothes holes' are you wearing (arm, neck, belt, buttonholes, decorative)? Investigate who in the class is wearing the most holes.
- Use a peg board to make 'pegs and holes' patterns (one peg - two holes - one peg...) Can a friend continue your sequence?
- Sort 'holey' objects or pictures by the size of hole, or the number of holes.
- Which plane or solid shapes fit together without leaving holes?
- Are all holes round? Draw and label the shapes of holes you can find in classroom objects.

Science
- Investigate how water comes out of holes (trickle, gush, spray). Try using bottles, strainers, holey yoghurt pots...
- How can you stop water running out of a sieve or flower pot?
- Do all holey things sink? Investigate.
- Choose five holey objects, e.g. spoon, bucket, spade, sieve, tube. Find out which is the most efficient for digging in sand.
- Draw a picture of yourself and label all the body holes. Can you say what they are for?
- Investigate the holes you can make in a piece of paper using different tools: nail, screw, fork, pencil, stick, straw. Which tools made large/small holes; smooth/ragged holes?

Art and Craft/Technology
- Cut out a tile shape from Plasticine, dough or clay. Use the end of a pencil to imprint an interesting holey pattern.
- Use 'holey' printers (cogs, cotton reels, washers) to decorate strips of paper 30cm long. Use these to make paper chains that link in different ways.
- Cut out a shape with holes in it (like a snowflake pattern) and use as a stencil over which to brush paint.

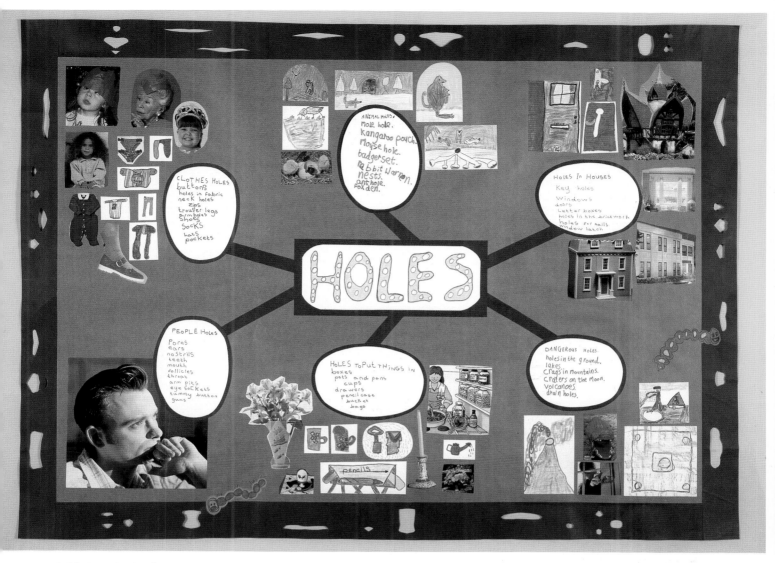

- Make a lacing/sewing card: use old greeting cards (or cut out magazine pictures stuck on card) and punch holes around the picture's outline.

- **Use strips of paper or card to make and decorate bangles** with a holey theme.

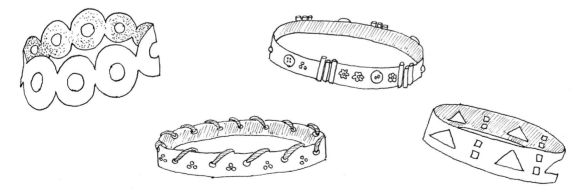

- Make a piggy bank from junk/construction toys. How will you get the money out again?
- Make a 'post the shape' game: cut holes in a junk box just the right size to post plane or solid shapes.

Hall time
- Play 'Mole in the hole'. In small groups: one child is the mole, the rest of the group form a 'hole' for him/her to creep through (leg tunnels, arm loops, body arches). Can mole go through without touching anybody?

- Target practice: throw beanbags/balls through a hand-held hoop.

Lines

Starters

What sorts of lines do the children know about: washing/fishing lines, telephone cables, lines on television, in books? Brainstorm words associated with lines such as patterning on the children's clothing: who is wearing stripy, zig-zag, wavy lines?

English

● On strips of paper, write the opening lines of some favourite stories. Can others match the lines to the stories?
● Give the children the closing line of a story, e.g. 'I take my skipping rope everywhere now, just in case.' Ask them to show the sequence of events leading up to this.
● **Draw a wiggly line and write words on it to describe its shape and movement.**

● Draw five children standing in the dinner line. Show in thought bubbles what they might be thinking as they wait for their meal.
● Make up a headline for a favourite story, e.g. 'ANANSI TRICKS AGAIN!'

Maths

● Draw along the side of different objects. Which give straight/curved lines? Sort them onto a Venn diagram.
● Make a time-line, placing members of the family in order from youngest to oldest.
● Pin four geo-strips together. Pull them out into a straight line and measure it. Push it into a zig-zag line. Estimate, then measure, how long the path is now.
● **Make two lines cross on a peg board.** How many different crosses can you make?

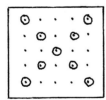 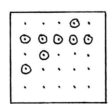 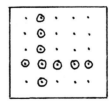

● Fold a piece of paper, open it out and record how many fold lines and regions you have made. Fold again and record.
● Measure the longest/shortest line you can make with five children.
● Draw a probability line showing what you are unlikely, likely, certain to do after school.

Science

● Look very carefully at the lines on friends' faces as they smile or frown. Draw their expressions, focusing on lines around the mouth, eyes and forehead.
● Take some rubbings from natural objects: wood, leaf, feather, shell. Are any of these lines straight?
● Is it true that no two finger prints are the same? Look at the similarities and differences in line patterns. Can you find a way of grouping these prints?
● Can you get a simple boat-shape (polystyrene or foil tray, toy boat) to move in a straight line across the water tray?

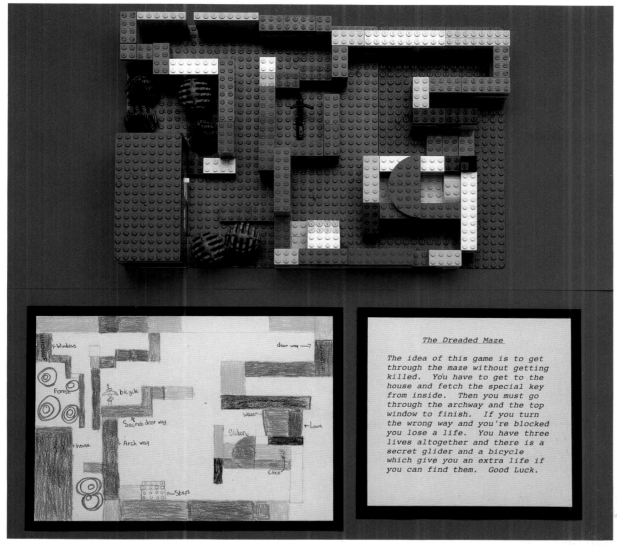

The Dreaded Maze

The idea of this game is to get through the maze without getting killed. You have to get to the house and fetch the special key from inside. Then you must go through the archway and the top window to finish. If you turn the wrong way and you're blocked you lose a life. You have three lives altogether and there is a secret glider and a bicycle which give you an extra life if you can find them. Good Luck.

Make a maze with Lego

Art and Craft
- Print with the side of a ruler to make a 'crossed lines' pattern. Fill in the spaces with more detailed line patterns.

- **Make a 'lines' sculpture.** Cut some strips of card. Cut two or three slots along the sides of each strip. Use these as interlocking sections to build into a 3D silhououette.

- Cut notches at intervals along the side of a wax crayon. Use this edge to make line patterns.
- Draw and cut out a large plane shape. Cut it into sections using straight lines. Gently spread them apart to 'explode' the shape.

Music
- Show the shapes of tunes by using hands to trace the rising and falling line patterns of a song: Hot Cross Buns (high, low, in between), Three Blind Mice (three steps down).
- Draw some simple line scores for the children to sing. Show lines rising up, sliding down, staying on one level, moving up and down in steps.

Hall time
- Play 'Follow my leader', making curved, looped or straight pathways; open and closed shapes.
- Play relay games to reinforce the idea of 'team lines'. Try slalom courses with teams running (or hopping, skipping) in zig-zag lines; or, jumping from side to side over ropes lined up in front of each team.

Marking time

Starters
Brainstorm words associated with the passage of time: before, after, during, bed/bath/meal times, days of the week, months, year. What sorts of things do we use to help us keep track of the time? Share experiences of the children's special times: birthdays, swimming on Fridays, festivals.

English
- Show the sequence of how you get ready for school in the mornings. Cut out and jumble the individual frames and ask a friend to reorder them.
- Draw three frames and describe what you did yesterday, are doing today, might do tomorrow.

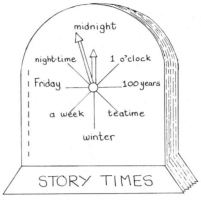

- **Describe and illustrate how time features in favourite nursery rhymes and stories.** Sleeping Beauty slept for 100 years; the Hungry Caterpillar ate for a week; the clock struck one.

- Make a zig-zag book showing how you would like to spend your half-term holiday week. Start each page: 'On Monday I will..; On Tuesday I will...'
- Describe what might happen if you had no way of telling the time. You might be late for school, miss the bus or doctor's appointment, arrive after the shop has shut.

Maths
- Count and chart how many pegs you can put in a peg board (cubes in a tower; beads you can thread) in one minute.
- Who gets up first in your family? Show this in a time sequence from earliest to latest.
- Survey who in the class has a watch. How could you show which are digital?
- Make picture sets of timers, e.g. watches, car/cooker/video clocks. Sort by whether: it hangs on the wall; has an alarm/digital display; can be worn.
- Chart the things you do every day (eat, walk the dog). What about weekly events such as swimming, library, Brownies? Can the children think of any monthly/yearly occasions?
- Have a time quiz. Invite the children to devise some questions for each other: 'What time is dinner?' 'How long is morning play?' 'Name the weekend days.' 'Name the third month.'

Science/Technology
- Which materials dry out the quickest? Wet some sponge, stone, sand, clay, wood, foil, cotton wool. Record the order in which they dry out. Was it a fair test?
- Look carefully at variations in the weather over one day. Record at regular intervals changes in things like: wind strength, cloud shape, full/partial sun.
- Make a badge to mark a special occasion in your year such as a birthday or festival.
- **Devise a game that involves using a sand timer.**

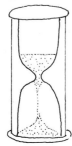 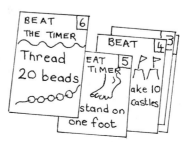

- Make an appointment card for a hairdresser (dentist/vet). Include lines for the day, month, year, and time.

Humanities

● Make a time-line showing the development from baby, toddler...grandparent.
● Can the children recall and recount an incident when they felt they had to wait for a long time?
● Chart where you can find clocks around the school.
● Work out the quickest route from your class to another room in school. Show which rooms, or significant features (store cupboard, cloakroom) you pass on the way.
● Record the month in which you were born on a time-line. Is everyone who was born in the same month, the same age now?

Music

● Investigate and set instruments that make long/sustained sounds (triangle, chime bars, cymbals), and shorter sounds (guiro, castanets). How can you make a long sound shorter?
● Take turns around a circle to clap four steady beats: each child follows on without leaving pauses between the sets of four. Try adding knee slaps/foot taps to the pattern.

Hall time

● Play 'Time's up': lay out 12 hoops as a large 'clock' face. The children step clockwise in and out of the hoops. On hearing 'TIME'S UP!' they must freeze. Whoever is in the l2 o'clock hoop (or other chosen time) is out.
● What is the quickest way to travel over 30m? In teams, try comparing walking, skipping or hopping times.

Monsters

Starters
What do the children think of when you say the word 'monsters' to them? Recall and describe the sorts of monsters they have come across and where they saw them: books, comics, magazines, cereal packets, snacks. Are monsters real or imaginary? Do you like them? Are they always scary?

English
● Make an alphabet of words for describing monsters: **a** for angry, **b** for bald, etc.
● Write a monster menu of foods starting only with 'm'. Give it a fantastical flavour: marshmallow, melon, mountains.
● Compile a 'Name your Baby' book for monsters. Are the names like ours? Try using onomatopoeia.
● Invent a monster language. Try adding a squeak at the end of a sentence, or the sound 'ee' to the end of each word. Will they be nonsense words, or just fun to say?
● Describe what everyday objects are to a monster who has never seen these things before.
● Show in a thought bubble what your initial reaction might be if you saw a monster in the playground. Are you startled, amused, or used to it? What might the monster think about you?

Maths
● Use link bricks to make a family of monsters: small, medium and large. Older children can construct models twice or three times as big.

● **Draw the different monster faces you can make using three circles, four squares, five triangles.**

● Draw and describe your monster mathematically: 'It has two eyes; it is six years old; there are five in the family; it can jump 300 metres; it is the third fastest runner in the universe...'
● Cut out a monster's footprint. Estimate, then measure, how many will fit along a cupboard or across the hall. Do the same for your own footprint and compare the two measurements.
● Draw a monster with one head, two arms, three legs. How does its appearance change shape as you place a mirror in different positions on the drawing?
● Use a sheet of newspaper to make a monster's shape just large enough for you and four friends to stand in.
● Make a Plasticine monster and weigh it. Change its shape (without adding or taking away any Plasticine). Estimate, then weigh again. Does a change in shape ever indicate a change of weight?

Science/Humanities
● Make a spotter's guide for a particular monster. Include information about: size, skin/fur/scales; where it lives; what it eats; day/night creature.
● Use construction toys or Plasticine to make a monster's habitat. Label features such as: hill, river, shore, cave, trees, buildings.
● Make a list of characteristics which 'prove' that your monster is a living thing (eats, sleeps, breathes, etc.). Compare these characteristics to your own.
● What might the alien's reaction be to seeing your playground for the first time? Would he think it: tidy, welcoming, boring?

Bubble-print some monsters

Art and Craft/Technology
● Make a monster mask or head band.
● Use squared paper to design a monster motif for a knitted jumper.
● Make a collage monster. Select appropriate materials for horns, shiny eyes, claws, etc.
● Design a stamp for your monster's land. Is it monster-shaped? What coinage does it use?
● **Use card to make a monster** with arms and legs that move.

Music
● Choose two musical instruments (e.g. guiro, tambour) and make up a musical conversation between two monsters. Do they speak slowly or quickly? In a regular or random pattern?
● Take the children for a journey round the monster landscape. Use instruments to make the sounds of the monster plodding up the hill, scurrying down, wading through a swamp, flying over a ravine.

Hall time
● Move that monster: give the children a very simple oral description of a monster: flapping ears/wings, spiny back, long tail. In small groups, the children make themselves into this monster shape. Try making it plod, scuttle, dance.

Moving About

Starters

Discuss how we move about: parts of the body; travelling from one place to another. Identify some classroom objects that move. How many movement words can the children tell you - up/down, sideways, swing...? What can the children tell you about how animals move?

English

- Write a movement poem. Each line describes a movement the children can make ('I can jump over...skate on...'). End each verse with the refrain 'Watch me move!'
- Move words around in a sentence stand - which moves change the meaning? For example, Sharaz sat on an elephant/an elephant sat on Sharaz. Which moves make nonsense?
- Describe and illustrate how animals move: trot, gallop, slither, slide, crawl, swoop. Put some ideas together in a 'Moving About' book.
- **Make a cartoon strip** showing what happens when a chair, or shoe, comes alive and starts moving about.

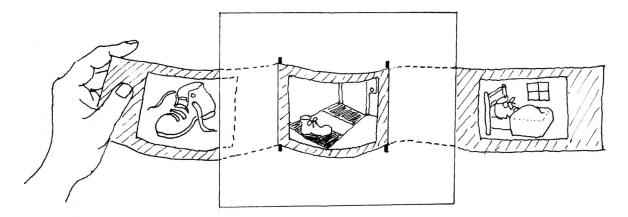

- Make a form for the 'Rest Easy Removal Co.' to help organise where to pick up/deliver goods. Include headings and spaces for: addresses, times, date, any special requirements (fragile goods, pets).

Maths

- Survey and sort things in the class that move: up and down, round and round, in and out.
- Make sets of things that move over land, through water or air.
- Investigate how solid shapes move. Chart which roll, slide, move in straight/curved pathways.
- Estimate, then count, how many steps up and down (or skips/jumps) you can do in one minute.
- Make a peg move from one side of the board to the other. Chart how many moves you make in your shortest/longest route.
- Trace and measure the pathways of things that move: handle, drawer, box lid, clock hands.
- Try turning yourself through whole, one half, one quarter, three quarter turns. Draw round a set toy to show the change of position as it moves through these same turns.

Science

- Draw a picture of yourself and label the parts that move: arms, eyes, fingers, elbows, toes. Do they all move in the same way? Which move up and down; round and round?
- Make a chart showing when you push or pull as you're putting on your clothes. Push feet into shoes, pull the laces, push head through neck hole, pull on a hat.
- Investigate the patterns you can make by using your hands in water. Can you move the water without touching it with your hands? Try blowing; or use a stick, fan, straw, whisk.
- Can you make a toy car move faster? Test using a gentle/hard push; pulling it along with string; slopes of various gradients.

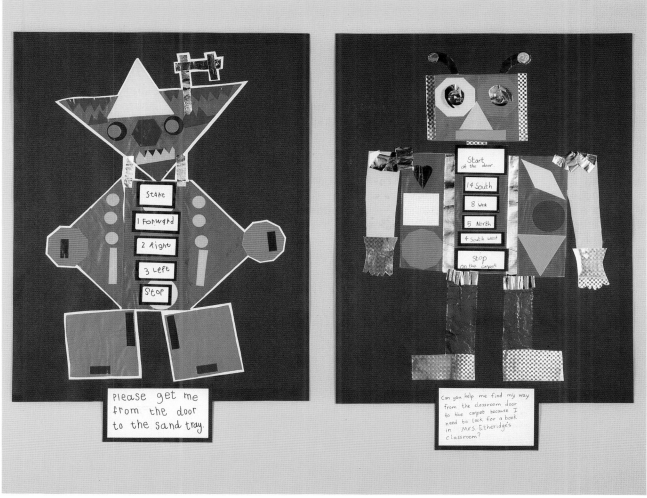

Please get me from the door to the sand tray.

(Robot display text: Start / 1 Forward / 2 Right / 3 Left / Stop)

Can you help me find my way from the classroom door to the carpet because I need to look for a book in Mrs. Etheridge's classroom?

(Robot display text: Start at the door / 14 South / 8 West / 5 North / 4 South West / Stop on the carpet)

Program a robot to move from place to place

Art and Craft/Technology
- Dribble glue in snake-like movement patterns on the paper. While still wet, drop sawdust, sand, or powder paints along the glue trail.
- Try finger painting different movement patterns: a smooth flowing river; the short quick movements of a machine.
- Make a pull-along trolley from construction toys to give a soft toy a ride.
- Use card and butterfly pins to make a jointed teddy or robot.
- **Make some pop-up characters.**

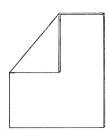 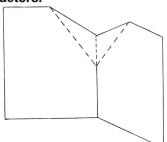 

Music
- What sorts of sounds do machines make as they move? Experiment with vocal sounds (ssh, glug glug, wheeee, spt, ch). Use a conductor to start your machine up slowly, make it go faster, slow down, stop and start up again.
- Sing 'If you're happy and you know it'. Add your own movement/body sounds to the song.

Hall time
- Move a beanbag (ball/quoit) across the hall. Set challenges: use only knees (backs, heels); balancing it on different parts of the body; working in pairs with feet/legs/backs touching.
- Mime moving through: a swamp, snowdrift, a plate of jelly, the sea, magic bubbles.

Newspaper

Starters
Which local/national newspapers do the children receive at home? Do they have a different paper at weekends? Where do we buy our newspapers (street vendors, newsagent etc.)? Discuss the various elements contained in newspapers: title, price, photographs, television listings, cartoons, stories etc. (see display photograph).

English
- Choose a photograph and add a speech bubble showing what the people/animals might be saying. Do their facial expressions give you any clues?
- Take a headline and put it into lower case letters, adding capitals only when necessary for proper nouns.
- Look at a photograph and add a caption to sum up the picture. Older children could look at the original headline and suggest an alternative.
- Look at names of various newspapers and make up an appropriate title for a class/school paper.

- **Advertise your local paper on a poster.**
  Use words and letters cut from newspapers for the text.

Maths
- Use a crayon or felt-tip pen to draw round shapes found in a sheet of newspaper, e.g. text columns, cartoon frames or weather charts. What do the children notice about these shapes?
- Mix up the pages and reassemble them in correct number sequence - try it against the clock.
- Cut out headlines and order them by length - does the longest strip always have the most words?
- Measure: the length/width of a page, width of a column, height of letters.

- **Cut out some story columns, crosswords and photographs.** Rearrange them on a tabloid-sized piece of paper. What is the most/least number of pieces you can fit on?

- Look at the prices of newspapers. Order them by price. Work out the cost of a particular newspaper for a day, week, month. How many can you get for £1, £2, £5 ?

Humanities
- Make a time-line by putting newspapers into date order.
- Sort newspapers into local/elsewhere; or daily/evening/weekly press.
- Use photographs as 'clue spotters'. How many things can the children discover from a picture? Consider, for example: Is it now/long ago? Are the people old/young? What might they be feeling? What was the weather like when the picture was taken?
- Cut out weather symbols from newspapers and make your own key, explaining what they mean.
  List places in order of temperature, from highest to lowest.

Art and Craft/Technology

● Make a torn newspaper picture of, for example, a person, newsagent's shop front or delivery van. Fill in extra details with a felt-tip pen.

● Paint a black and white picture to illustrate a headline, e.g. 'RECORD HARVEST', 'FLOODED OUT'.

● **Use a sheet of newspaper** to make a nurse's, pirate's or cook's costume to fit yourself, or a friend.

● Use newspapers to make a delivery bag, with shoulder straps. Is it strong enough to hold three newspapers?

● Make a newsagent's rack to hold four newspapers. Make sure the titles can all be seen.

Music

● Clap and say the names of newspapers rhythmically. Have any papers the same pattern (Daily Star - Daily Mail, etc)?

● Make sounds with hand movements on a sheet of newspaper. Try making both short sounds (tap, flick, slap) and long (stroke, nail scrapes). In a circle, take turns to make long/short sounds in as many different ways as possible.

● In small groups, play a crossword. With an instrument each, children choose to be the black or white squares. 'Conduct' the players by pointing to the squares in sequence.

Hall time

● Newspaper wolf: adapt the familiar game of 'What's the time, Mr. Wolf?' to ask instead: 'What are you reading, Mr. Wolf?' Everyone is safe when the replies are 'reading a book' (comic, poster, recipe etc.), but are chased when the wolf says 'READING A NEWSPAPER'.

● Use a rolled up newspaper as a baton in relay races.

Numbers all Around

Starters

Brainstorm situations and places where the children meet numbers in their daily lives - at school/home, out and about. Which numbers have they seen or used so far today: alarm clock, clothes sizes, bus/car numbers, dials, registers, dinner money? Talk about 'personal numbers' (see Humanities).

English
● Illustrate and caption some favourite number rhymes. Try your own versions, e.g. 'Ten green bottles' becomes 'Ten blue balloons hanging in a shop, One gets accidentally popped...'
● List the titles of stories where numbers are central: the Three Bears, Millions of Cats, etc. Try arranging the contents list (from lowest to highest numbers) for a 'Numbers in Stories' guide.

● **Write the recipe for your favourite snack,** highlighting the numbers used.

● Spot the numbers in non-fiction books: page numbers, ISBN, publication date, library classification, date stamps. Make a glossary of these numbers.
● It's the grand draw at the summer fair and you're holding the winning ticket! Show in speech bubbles what was said as your number was called out.

Maths
● List the children's house numbers. How many have one, two or three digits? Order them on a number line.
● Chart all the shoe sizes worn in your class. Can you order them from smallest to largest? What do you notice about the number pattern?
● Investigate the different ways measurements are shown on clothing: chest/waist, age ranges, small/medium/large.
● Sort junk boxes by looking at how the contents are measured: kilo, grams, pints, quantity.
● Make a set of digital figures from link bricks, matchsticks or rods.
● How many numbers can you spot from 1-100 in and around the class? Colour them in on a number square as you find them. Investigate: page/door numbers, pieces in game boxes, tape-counters.
● Draw, or find pictures of, measuring equipment used at home/school: ruler, scales, speedometer, thermometer, clock.

Humanities
● Make a personal number history. Record information such as age, door/car/telephone number; number of family members.
● Which adults work with numbers in school? Show how the secretary, cook, cleaner use numbers in their work.
● Write directions for a friend to follow to get from the table to the home corner. Use instructions such as: four paces left, two right (or five paces north, three east).
● How many numbers can you spot around the school that give you clues about how old things are (sell-by dates on junk boxes, the register, school commemorative plaque)? List these numbers and record where you found them.

Art and Craft/Technology
● Make a montage using numbers cut from pictures of car number plates, clocks, door numbers, etc.
● Draw a large bubble number and embellish it to create a fantastical character or animal.

1 bow 2 snails 3 sandcastles

4 candles 5 balloons 6 flowers

Make a tactile number frieze

● **Cut out a card number stencil** and use
it to design interesting patterns.

● Make an age badge showing your present age.

● **Make some number dominoes.** Use any combination of figures, pictures and words
to illustrate the numbers.

Music
● Sing some popular number rhymes. Encourage the children to join in with instruments on the number
words, e.g. One, two, buckle my shoe; One potato, two potato...
● Set up a steady pulse of four beats (knee slap, clap, clap, clap), with everyone joining in. Keeping the beat
steady, take it in turns to say your name on the 'knee slap'. Try using three or two beats. Change the body
sounds.

Hall time
● Play 'Numbers are go'. Ask the children to skip around, listening for the command 'FREEZE!' Then call out
any number from 2-10. The children should get into groups of that particular number as quickly as
possible. Break groups and skip around again until the next 'FREEZE!' command when you call out
another number. Try: calling out 'odd' or 'evens' or 'half the class'.

Old Mother Hubbard

Starters
Encourage the children to join in with the rhyme and help them to fix the story line in their minds. Look for clues to establish that the setting is historical rather than contemporary. Who amongst people close to them, do the children consider old? (For full versions of the rhyme see Resources, page 72).

English
● Brainstorm other pairs of rhyming words and link them in an amusing sentence (see display photograph).
● Make a picture-word dictionary to help the children understand some of the key words in the rhyme (jig, tripe, hatter...). Older children could use a dictionary or write their own simple definitions.

● **Retell the story as Mother Hubbard's shopping list.** Show the shops and what she bought there.

● Show, in a speech bubble, Mother Hubbard's reaction to her dog's funny antics - is she surprised, amused, matter of fact?
● Focusing on action words, make a sequel to the rhyme showing other bizarre things the dog might get up to (digging a hole...baking a cake...)
● Draw/cut out and label 4 or 5 items you would find in the tailor's shop (barber's, hatter's) and use as picture riddles to guess 'Where is Mother Hubbard now?'

Maths
● Carry out a survey to find out if dogs are the most popular pets.
● Draw/cut out pictures to make sets showing what you might find in kitchen/bedroom/bathroom cupboards.
● Draw/tally the number and kind of plane shapes found in classroom cupboards or low storage units.
● Make up a probability line for a dog. Draw four things showing what is impossible, unlikely, likely, certain that a dog could do.

● **On squared paper, draw different shaped 'cupboards' to hold twelve cubes without wasting space (6x2, 4x3, 12x1).**

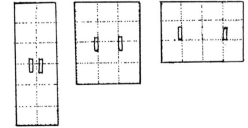

● Where am I in the cupboard? Line up sorting toys or Logi Blocks. Take turns to find the toy by describing its position (first, second, middle, left, right) and attributes (thick/thin, red/square).

Humanities
● Ask the children to make a picture inventory of their drawer/tray. Older children could give more detailed descriptions, e.g. one metal sharpener; a car with only one wheel...

● Who do the children consider to be 'old' - relations/known adults? **Make a generation diagram.**

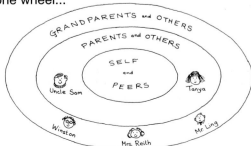

A goat in a coat.

A nurse in a purse.

A cat in a hat.

A bug on a rug.

A flower in a shower.

A dog on a cog.

- Show where you could buy some of Mother Hubbard's purchases nowadays, e.g. coats from: department stores, supermarkets, mail order, catalogues, Nearly New. Which of these could Mother Hubbard have used?
- Think about keys on a map. Make picture symbols for each of the shops visited by Mother Hubbard (scissors for the barber; needle/thread for the tailor...)

Art and Craft/Technology
- Wax resist a picture of one of the dog's antics.
- Take rubbings in different colours. Cut out shapes from the rubbings sheets to make a picture of Mother Hubbard in her bonnet/long apron.
- Make yourself a wig on a headband/hat shape. Cover with curled paper, wool, polystyrene chips.
- Use construction toys to make Mother Hubbard's shopping basket: try adding handles, a lid or wheels.
- Make the dog's dish from junk and decorate with a Mother Hubbard theme.
- Make a cupboard out of a box. Incorporate simple hinges on the doors, and some shelves.

Music
- Sing the rhyme to the traditional tune (see Resources, page 72). Try fitting the words to other familiar tunes, e.g. 'Little Bo Peep'.
- Make up some jig music for the dog to dance to. Establish some dance rhythms on instruments, e.g. hop (woodblock taps), skip (skipping rhythms on triangle), twirl (tambourine shake). Make up a jig sequence using these. Can others dance to the music, changing their steps as the instruments change?

Hall time
- Play 'Shop stop': divide the class into four teams representing different shops (baker, newsagent, butcher, greengrocer). Set out four 'shops' (mats) in a big circle and allocate each team to one of these mats. Call out an item which can be bought from one of the shops, e.g. BREAD. The 'bakers' then run round all the mats. Last back to their shop mat is out. Keep going until all the shops are bare.

Opposites

Starters
How many opposites can the children spot on themselves? Who is wearing patterned/plain clothes; thick/thin belts; long/short sleeves? Play a game where the children must do the opposite of what you say: 'sit down' (class stands up); 'clap quickly' (slow claps).

English
● Make a menu of cold food you would like to eat on a hot summer's day. What about hot food for cold days?
● Draw the covers for, or list titles/authors of, five fact and five fiction books.
● Write a story sequence involving a magical 'opposite' change, e.g. shrinking and growing; travelling quickly/slowly.
● Choose a category such as television programmes (or games, clothes) and list your personal likes/dislikes.
● Write a simple sentence, e.g. 'The sad clown walked down the road.' Spot the opposites and change the sentence to read 'The happy clown ran up the road.'

Maths
● Find pairs of long/shorter objects from, for example, the book corner, crayon box, play house, junk trolley. Older children can measure the difference between the pairs.
● Collect data to find out who is the tallest/shortest in the class.
● Take five objects and sort them onto a decision tree, answering yes/no to questions like: is it blue, does it roll, has it got wheels?

● **Make a sequence using opposites**
(large/small, pointing up/down, heads/tails).
Can a friend spot the opposites used?

● Throw a dice and record how often you get odd or even numbers in 10/15/20 throws.
● Take five cars (or farm animals). Line them up facing left. Order and label them first...to last. Reorder the line to face right and label the new positions.

Science
● Sort objects by using pairs of opposites: rough/smooth; shiny/dull; soft/hard.
● Draw two pictures - a daytime and a night-time scene. Label them, thinking about: dark and light; people and their activities; animals; buildings.
● Make a poster highlighting how to be safe in dangerous situations. Think about using matches, boiling water, plugs, fireworks, medicines.
● Make a table showing which objects are, and are not, attracted to magnets.

Art and Craft/Technology
● Wet and dry pictures: paint a teddy on dry paper. Paint another on wetted paper - how different do the two teddies look?
● Use small and large printers to make straight and wavy line patterns.

● **Make an opposites matching game**:
fold and cut paper like this: Make careful
drawings showing pairs of opposites - can
a friend guess what is under the flaps?
(See photograph.)

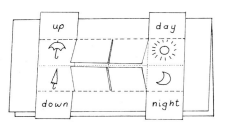

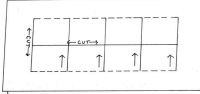

● Mix up some light and dark blues. Use these shades to finger-paint stormy/calm seascapes.

● Make an 'in and out' thaumatrope, e.g. fish in
a tank; a swimmer in the sea; a dog in a basket.

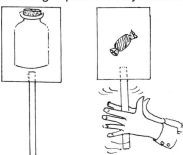

Music
● Sit opposite a partner. One person plays an instrument in a certain way, and says how she/he is playing it (quickly, heavily, loudly). The person opposite then has to play in the opposite manner (slowly, lightly, softly).
● Sing the 'Hokey Cokey' incorporating as many opposites as you can into verses of your own: face to the front/back; stand up high/crouch down low; hands open/closed; voice quiet/loud.

Hall time
● Dips: in pairs, tap opposite hands, knees, shoulders. Try making a sequence for others to copy.
● Opposite Stations: in 'train' groups of four (one driver, three trucks, all linked), children chug around the hall listening for the command 'SIDINGS!' They must then find another 'train' to stand opposite. When each group has found another train to stand opposite, give the 'ALL CLEAR!' signal to move off again.

Our School

Starters
What sorts of information do the children think visitors to their school would find especially useful? How will they find their way around? What class/school routines would it be helpful to identify - play/lunch/hall times?

English
- Make an name list to help take turns on the computer or remember table groups.
- Show the sequence of your early morning class routines, e.g. hang up coat > change book > put snack in box > sit on the carpet.
- Practise saying/writing your school address - try putting it to a tune.
- Make an individual ID card showing your portrait and information such as: name, age, class, hair/eye colour (see display photograph).
- Ask the children to draw and caption some useful reminders to help you get organised around the class: 'Only 3 in the play house please'; ' Have you labelled your snack?' (See display photograph.)
- Make a 'Who's Who?' directory for key school personnel (head, secretary, cook, dinner/class helpers). Draw their portraits and list information such as: name, when they are in school, where you can find them, what they do.
- Make a poster emphasising key commands for your fire drill: STAND STILL, LISTEN TO YOUR TEACHER, WALK.

Maths
- Make a timetable as a sequence of pictures or a chart. Show important times in the day/week. Include things like: play, dinner, home time, assembly, quiet reading.
- **Chart class activities (and behaviour) showing which you do sometimes, often, never.**

- Make a survey of which class activities are most popular. Show on a mapping diagram or bar chart, how many people prefer the wet area, writing corner, problem solving, music.
- Have you enough straws for today's milk drinkers? What about tomorrow, the rest of the week?

- **Find a useful way of showing the teacher who is having packed/school lunches; going home for lunch.**

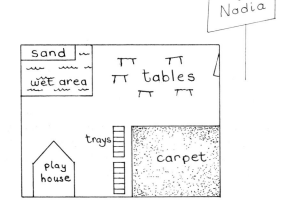

Humanities
- Draw the outside of the school and label features such as: windows, playground, wheelchair ramp, steps.
- Survey how we travel to school (walk, bus, car). Draw any landmarks you pass on the way (Post Office, bridge, park) to help others find your school.

- **Draw a simple picture map of the main areas of your classroom: carpet, tables, wet area.**

Try putting some activities together in a book for visitors, new pupils or supply teachers

- Write simple directions (or make a footprint route) showing how to get from your class to the library (hall, playground). For example, 4 steps right, 3 steps left...
- Put an entry in the visitors book showing who came and what they might have done (school nurse, Rabbi, community police officer, plumber).

Art and Craft/Technology
- Make some reward badges to use in class, e.g. 'Well done!', 'You tried hard', 'I listened well' (see photograph).
- Make a welcome banner - how many scripts, languages and different ways of saying 'Hello, Welcome' can you incorporate?
- Use chalk or wax to make a portrait of the school cook (secretary, caretaker).
- Design a logo for a new school sweat shirt.
- Paint the view looking out from a school window or door.
- Draw a game you know (or devise a new one) which your school might be able to paint on the playground, e.g. target games, number tracks, grids.

Hall time
- Mime aspects of the school day: milk, lunch, story time; or jobs (caretaker, secretary).
- Play 'In time'. Make a corridor down the centre of the hall with beanbags. Explain that this represents the wall separating inside from outside. The children run a circuit round the beanbags, listening for the command 'IN TIME!', when they must freeze. Those on the corridor side are 'home'; those standing on the playground side miss one turn.

Puzzle it Out

Starters
Get the children into the 'puzzle it out' and problem-solving mood by playing a game of 'Guess Who?' Encourage them to deduce which child (number, season) you are thinking of, by asking questions to which you will only answer yes or no.

English
- Can you say/write some clues for a friend to puzzle out which story book you are thinking about? For example, 'It's about three bears and one of them stays up all night...'

- **Make a deliberate mistake in a nursery rhyme,** e.g. 'Little Bo Peep has lost her cat.' Illustrate the captions and compile into a class puzzle book.

- Puzzle out your own captions to a picture book which has no text.
- A magician has turned your friend into a rabbit. Puzzle out what you should put in a magic recipe to undo the spell.
- Jumble up the letters of some simple words (dog - ogd). Can your friend puzzle them out?
- Cut out magazine/catalogue pictures. Add a speech bubble and puzzle out what the characters might be saying.

Maths
- Record how many different sized squares you can make on a geo-board or peg board.

- **Take six linking bricks in assorted colours** and fit them together while your friends shut their eyes. Can they puzzle out how to make one the same while you describe it to them?

- How many different ways can you get a score of five, using two dice? Try other totals.
- How many dominoes have a difference of 1 (6:5; 3:2...) Make sets of dominoes with differences of 2,3,4. Which set is the largest - why?
- A sweet shop sells chews in two shapes and three colours. How many different chews could you buy?
- Using only the keys l. 2. 3. + on the calculator, try to make all the numbers from 0 - 9. Record what you did. Compare these with a friend. Were there any numbers you could not make?

Humanities
- Give picture or word clues to describe somebody's job in school - can others puzzle out who it is?
- Choose three objects (book, soft toy, box) and draw the bird's eye view of one of these - can a friend match your drawing to the object?
- Draw, or use construction toys, to make a roadway with some junctions. Think about how you can make it safe to cross the road (bridge, zebra/pelican crossing, lollipop person).
- Hide a piece of 'treasure' and make a trail for a friend to puzzle out where it is hidden. Try foot prints, paper arrows, step-by-step instructions.

Technology
- Make a jigsaw using old greetings cards, magazine pictures or children's drawings. Experiment with the number of cuts. Make a container for it (box, bag, envelope, frame). (See display photograph.)

- Make a five-page puzzle book to keep you amused on a car journey. Include some of the following: colour by number; odd one out; word search; matching pairs, e.g. animals to their homes.
- Use Plasticine coils or construction toys to make a simple maze.
- Plan and draw a simple dot-to-dot puzzle which could be reproduced for the whole class.

- **Make a noughts and crosses board with some 3D counters.**

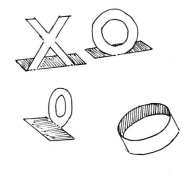
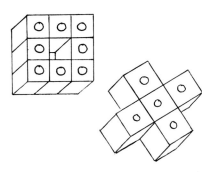

Music
- Tap out the rhythm of the first line of a favourite song - can others puzzle out what it is?
- Put the children into pairs facing each other, with three instruments in between them (triangle, tambour, wood blocks). Child A hides his eyes while child B plays one of the instruments - which one is it? Try playing two of the instruments together- puzzle out which have been used.

Hall time
- Solve it! Set challenges for individuals/groups to act out. How can you cross a river without a bridge (boat, stepping stones, swim); move a heavy box (push, pull with rope, van); clean a giant's boot?

Rainy Days

Starters
Brainstorm vocabulary describing varying degrees of rainfall: a gentle shower, downpour, cloudburst, torrential, drizzle, mizzle...Play with the sounds of 'Rainy day' words (drip drop, pitter-patter). What kinds of clothes are most suitable for rainy weather?

English
● Act out, or write, the local forecast for some rainy day conditions (see Starters).
● Draw a picture sequence or flow chart showing how to change out of rainboots and raincoats without getting your socks wet on the floor.
● Show in thought bubbles: 'If it wasn't raining I could be...(playing in my sand pit...)'
● Compile an alphabet of words associated with rainy days: anorak, blustery, clouds...
● Focusing on onomatopaeia, make up a rainy day tongue-twister: splish, splosh, splash...

Maths
● Sort or sequence rainboots by: colour, foot size, leg height, or sole pattern.
● Survey the outdoor clothes worn on a rainy day. Interpret the data: is most of the clothing waterproof? Who might have come by car, or missed the weather forecast?

● **Take two pairs of rainboots - how many different ways can you arrrange them?** Look for, and draw, reflections and rotations.

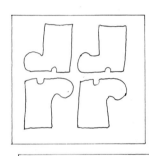
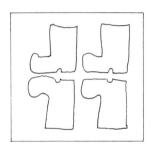
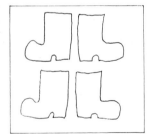

● Make a probability line showing things you are unlikely, likely, and certain, to be doing on a rainy day.
● Estimate, then measure, the length of everybody's rainboots placed end to end in a line.
● Are all materials heavier when wet? Compare the weight of fabrics dry, then wet.

Science/Humanities
● Which materials mop up drips under umbrellas/rainboots most efficiently - newspaper, fabric, sponge, grease-proof paper?
● Investigate the difference between 'water-proof' and 'shower-proof'. Record how many drops of water you can drip on to anoraks/umbrellas before it soaks through.

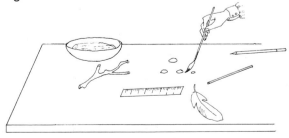

● **Make drips and drops on a table top.** Are all drops the same shape and size? What happens when two drops touch? Record your observations.

- Find, then plot on a simple map, the areas which are wet/dry around the school on a rainy day. Where would it be best to shelter?
- Look at weather chart symbols on class charts or in newspapers. Devise your own symbols for rainy conditions such as: thunderstorms, drizzle, squally showers.

Art and Craft/Technology
- Experiment with different ways of making 'rainy splashes': spatter prints, finger painting, printing with ruler edges.
- Paint or draw with felt-tipped pens on dampened paper.
- Make puddle-reflection pictures. Paint on one half of the paper, and fold over while the paint is still wet.
- Wax resist some colourful umbrellas.
- Design a rain hat for yourself, or a soft toy. Think about size, how to keep it on, making it look attractive, and waterproof.
- Plan the contents of a 'wet playtime' box. What would the children most like it to contain? Are there any playtime restrictions (no scissors, glue, Plasticine)?

Music
- Use instruments to make some rainy day music. Try a steady drizzle rhythm on tambourines. Use clave taps for water dripping off trees; shakers for rain gushing down drainpipes; drums for thunder rolls. Put some ideas into a sound sequence. Start with single heavy raindrops, make a sudden downpour, and gradually die away to a light 'drip, drop'.

Hall time
- Act out rainy day activities: pulling on raincoats, putting up umbrellas, splashing through puddles, avoiding splashes from buses, wringing out socks.
- Incy Wincy: have six 'spiders' in the middle of a class circle of 'raindrops'. Everybody says the rhyme. On the phrase 'washed the spider OUT', the raindrops must try to catch a spider.

String and Things

Starters
Who is wearing something today with string ties, ribbons, laces? What purpose do these serve? Which are just for decoration? Brainstorm associated vocabulary (see English). Apart from clothing, what else do we use stringy things for - washing lines, sewing, knitting, parcels, nets?

English
● Make a long string of vocabulary associated with the topic: rope, braid, ribbon, wool, lace, cord, raffia, cotton, tow-rope, shoe laces, fishing line.
● How could a favourite story character make good use of a piece of rope? For example, Hansel and Gretel could make a trail through the woods, climb down it, tie up the witch.
● Make a cartoon sequence: you start off with three items in your string shopping bag. Show how they fall out one by one on the way home. What does grandad say when you arrive empty-handed?
● Fill in the competition entry form on the back of a packet of ribbon. It asks you to show three different ways you used the contents. Was it for a hair decoration, rosette, or for tying a parcel?
● Make a 'String Surprises' lift-the-flap book (see display photograph). Brainstorm what the surprising piece of string could turn out to be - a dog's lead, yo-yo, shoe laces.

Maths
● Sort a collection of threads by: length, colour, patterning, flat/twisted, thickness.
● How many different objects can you find to thread on your string: button, air-flow ball, pencil grip?
● Draw a large figure 2 on a chalk board: estimate, then measure, how much cord you will need to trace its outline. Try other figures.
● How much ribbon is needed to make a bow to go round the neck of a soft toy?
● Use threads to measure the circumference of, for example, a ball, mug, jar, your waist/head.
● Draw a wiggly line on a piece of paper. Can you find the halfway mark?
● What length of string will you need to measure the height of everyone in the class?

Science
● Unravel some threads and chart how many separate strands you find. Investigate if the number of strands relates to the thickness of the thread.

● **Try using string to join two pieces of:** paper, plastic, fabric, polystyrene, wood, stone, metal. Show how you did it - were any especially difficult?

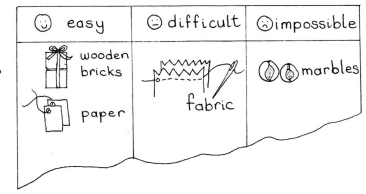

● Devise a test to find out which threads are most stretchy.
● How strong is thread? Try rubbing different threads against a rough surface. How many rubs until it breaks? Does it break cleanly, or does it fray?
● Try tying knots in a range of different threads. Chart which are easiest/impossible to untie.

Art and Craft/Technology
● Make a pattern lacing board by punching holes in a piece of card or polystyrene tray.
● Design and make a wool (or string/ribbon) dispenser to stop your threads getting all tangled up.
● Wrap threads around a box or piece of wood and use it as a printing block.
● Weave threads around two pieces of stick (or straws/card strips) fixed in a cross shape.

● **Style your own stringy self portrait.** Use
threads in different ways: coil, loop, plait, knot.

Hall time
● Enjoy some traditional skipping rhymes (see Resources, page 72), e.g. Salt, mustard, vinegar; Jelly on the plate; birthday months.
● Make closed shapes with ropes on the floor. Try: moving round them in heel-to-toe steps; placing hands in the middle of the shapes and 'walking' feet round; putting feet in the shapes and 'walking' on hands; jumping in and out.

Take Six

Starters
Ask the children to tell you everything they know about six. Encourage responses such as: 3 add 3 makes 6; I'm six soon; my brother takes size six shoes; six eggs in a box; I've got six letters in my name; my house number has six in it.

English
● The wizard has lost the potion that wakes him up at 6 o'clock. Which six things will he put in his new mixture? Older children could keep to the six theme: an insect, half-dozen eggs...
● Take the 6th letter of the alphabet: how many animals (toys, names, foods) can you think of before the timer runs out? Use a dictionary to help find more.
● List words starting with the same sound as six. Make some of these into nonsense alliterative phrases, e.g. six silly sausages singing solos.
● Make a poem with a six theme. Each line starts: 'I'd rather have..(six cream buns) than...(a piece of burnt toast); I'd rather have six legs than two...'
● List/draw in order of preference six things you would like to do on a visit to Grandma's.
● Choose up to six books and chart their 'star rating' from one (probably won't read it again) to six (brilliant!).

Maths
● Which six containers will hold six yoghurt pots of water without overflowing?
● Use geo-strips or a pin board to make six-sided shapes. You could go on to investigate whether any of these shapes tessellate (see display photograph).
● Take six coins (lp, lp, 2p, 2p, 5p, 5p). How many different values can you make using any combination of these coins?
● Chart how often the number six comes up when you throw a die 6, 12, 18, 24 times.

● **Use square/dotty paper to** find out how many different routes six units long you can make.

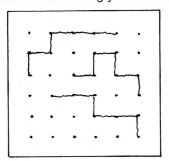 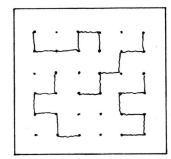

● One egg can be placed in six different positions in an egg box. Investigate and chart how you could place two in the box.
● Use a calculator to help you find different ways of making the answer six (10-4; 3+3; 12 DIVIDED BY 2).
● Find six places in/around the school where you can measure a length of six metres.

Science/Technology

● **Find six different ways of joining two pieces of paper together.** How can you make sure they stay together but can also be separated again without tearing?

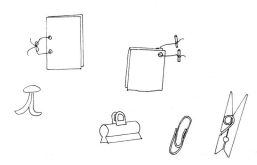

- Put six small objects (e.g. peg, paper clip, bead) in a box. Can you stop them rattling? How might newspaper, card strips, polystyrene, tape or Plasticine help?
- Make a wheeled vehicle to transport six Duplo bricks or Lego people.
- Decorate a card cut-out of the figure 6, and make it into a brooch to give a friend who will soon be six years old.
- Design a shoe lacing card with six holes to practise tying your laces.
- Make up a simple game which uses two dice. What happens when you throw a six, or double six?

Art and Craft
- Make an interesting arrangement of six classroom objects for the children to draw in 'still life'.
- Fasten six crayons together with an elastic band and use to experiment with different line patterns.
- Make six paper cylinders and arrange them as a tube sculpture.
- Make a tessellating pattern using a six-sided shape (see photograph).
- Fold a piece of paper into six frames. Mix six different tints of blue and put one in each frame.

Hall time
- Find six different places on the body to balance a beanbag/quoit.
- Find six different ways of moving a ball from A to B, e.g. with feet/hands only, roll, bounce.
- Run in and out of a six-post slalom; travel through a six-piece obstacle course.

The Three Billy Goats Gruff

Starters
Retell the story in your own words. How do the children respond to the troll - do they think he was simply greedy or easily tricked? Talk about what bridges are for. Have fun saying the 'trip trap' refrain in small, medium and large voices.

English
● Retell the story using simple props (goats, bridge, troll). Make sure the children know and use the refrain.
● Identify and sound out the **tr** blends in the story. Brainstorm some other **tr** words and display them on a troll shape.
● Draw and describe what you imagine the troll's home might look like - does it live under the bridge where it is cold and damp?
● Show in thought bubbles what the troll might be thinking in between meeting each goat, e.g. 'I'll wait for the bigger one...', 'I'm getting really hungry now...'
● Describe what you think might happen to the goats on the way back. Will the same trick work again? Will they decide to take a different route home?

Maths
● Find/draw objects which come in three different sizes (cubes, spoons, etc.). Younger children could order small, medium, large. Older children can make comparative measurements: the large spoon is...cm longer than...

● **Make several sets of three linking cubes.** Join them to make bridges of - 6, 9, 12, l5, 18 cubes. Draw and chart how many sets of three were used each time.

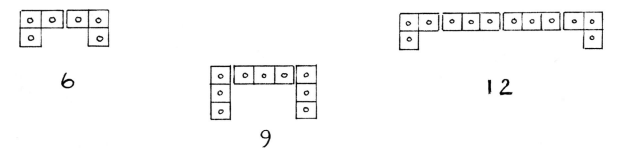

● How many different three-sided goat pens can you make using pin boards or geo-strips?
● Model the goats from three pieces of Plasticine (e.g. 100, 150, 200gm). Find objects which balance each goat. Which goat combinations can stand on a bridge supporting 300gm?
● Take a sheet of paper to represent a river. Cut and measure lengths of string (bridges) to cross the river. Are straight bridges always the quickest route across?

Humanities
● Show in a labelled picture your position in the family - start from the oldest family member.
● Why do we have bridges? Make sets of things that go over/under bridges. Are there any which travel both over and under?
● Make a simple picture map illustrating the story setting. Include: fields, hills, woodland, river, bridge. Describe some possible routes for the goats to travel from one side of the bridge to the other.
● Identify rivers and bridges on maps/atlas. How many place names can the children find which have bridge (ford/ferry) in them?

Art and Craft/Technology
● Use construction toys to make a simple troll (5-8 pieces). Draw pictures giving step-by-step instructions so a friend can make one just the same (see display photograph).
● Make a simple mask/headdress for the troll or a goat - use to help retell the story.

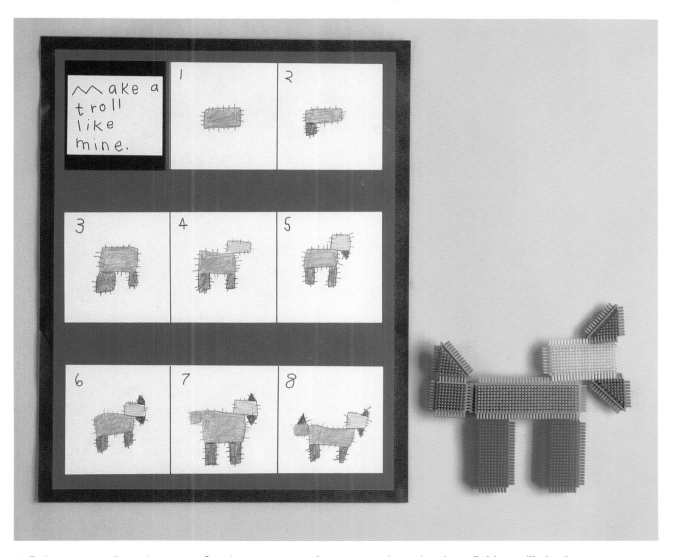

- Paint a scene from the story. Comb-scrape over features such as the river, fields, troll's body.
- Make bridge shapes to cross a river 50cm wide. Experiment with loose bricks, construction toys, rulers, paper.

- **Make a picture of the river and bridge joining two fields.** Draw the goats on card strips. Cut out slots for them to cross the bridge. Where could a troll pop up and surprise them?

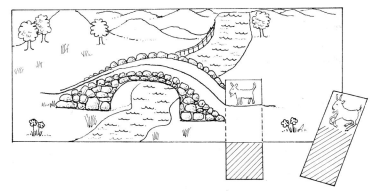

Music
- Try retelling the story with instruments. Use a guiro, tulip blocks or claves to represent the three goats 'trip trapping' over the bridge. Punctuate this rhythm with the troll's questioning sounds (tambour/drum). Play these elements against a continuous sound of the trickling river (glockenspiel) until the troll falls in the water with a big cymbal SPLASH!

Hall time
- Act out the story in groups of four: one troll and three billy goats.
- Stepping stones: put out enough hoops for two-thirds of the class. The children 'swim' in the river between the hoops, listening for the command 'TROLL'S COMING!' They must then find a hoop to jump into (one person only in each hoop). Gradually remove hoops until the last swimmer is left in the river.

Autumn Seeds and Leaves

COLLECT: tree seeds and leaves: cones (fir, lime, alder); winged (sycamore, ash, lime); nuts (acorn, conker, beech mast, walnut, chestnuts). Try to have some leaves and seeds from one type of tree. Children's reference books. Name labels for leaves and seeds; knife.

Starters
Play an 'it's Autumn' detective game in small groups. Mix up some leaves and ask each member of the group to select one to look at very closely for sixty seconds. Mix the leaves up again - can they identify which one was theirs? Wash hands after handling the collection.

English
● Do the leaf shapes remind the children of anything? Ask them to write descriptions such as: 'It's like a finger'. (a giant's hand, a spiky hedgehog's back).
● Write a label for the Autumn seeds and leaves display table. Give it an appropriate border.
● List words describing the movement/sound of leaves: twist, tumble, rustle, shuffle. Choose some of these words to make a simple poem written on leaf shapes falling across the page.
● Invent your own seed; describe its appearance and what sort of fantastical tree it might grow in to. Will it bear amazing colours, wishing fruits, cream buns?
● Write the squirrel's reminder note to describe where in the garden it's hidden a winter seed store.

Maths
● How many different ways can you find to sort seeds: prickly, smooth, winged, shiny?
● Put five conkers on a scale pan. Can you make them balance with five other conkers? Try balancing them with more/fewer conkers. Interpret your findings.
● Order leaves by length; or shades of colour from light to dark.

● **Compare the number of seeds found in different fruits** (conker, beech mast, ash key). Chart your findings by mapping the seed case to the seeds found inside, or make a bar chart.

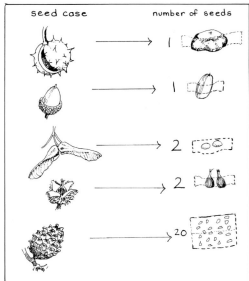

● Estimate/count how many conkers will fill a box. Try another seed - will you need more/fewer?
● Choose five leaves and place them end to end. Estimate, then measure, their length. Try with a different set of five leaves or seeds.
● Draw round a leaf and cut out its shape. Try folding it to find lines of symmetry.

Science
● Take a leaf rubbing and label some of the following: stalk, veins, midrib, smooth/jagged edges.
● Choose one seed case and make careful drawings of the outside and inside.
● Place six different seeds in a box - can you recognise them by touch alone?
● How dirty are leaves? Rub a leaf gently between folded tissue. Repeat using other leaves - can you order them from cleanest to dirtiest?
● Investigate which winged seeds travel furthest. Compare those with two wings, and one wing. Does size make a difference?
● Devise a test to find which conker would win a 'toughness championship'. Try: squeezing/stamping on it; or dropping it from a height until it breaks.

Make a poster using leaf spatter prints

Art and Craft
- Make leaf skeletons using straws, pipe cleaners, lace, paper cut-out patterns. String together as a mobile.
- Draw a hedgehog's 'home' and show how seeds and leaves could be incorporated into furnishings, e.g. winged-seed lamp shades; leaf curtains, acorn bowls.
- Blow-print the trunk and branches of a tree. Take prints of leaves to position on the branches.

- **Embellish a leaf rubbing with felt-tip pen**
  or crayons to make a hedgehog, monster
  or clown's spiky hair.

- Make a seed sculpture. Try using glue, cocktail sticks, or threads to hold the seeds together.

Hall time
- Autumn Days: ask the children to make seed body shapes (spiky, winged, smooth) and movements (sway, fall, spin, fly, drop, roll). Try a 'fun in the leaves' mime: stamp, shuffle, kick, scoop and throw, rake and sweep, build a bonfire.

Buttons

COLLECT: buttons in various colours, sizes, materials and with different numbers of holes and fastenings.

Starters
Talk to the children about where all these buttons may have come from. What sort of clothes do the children wear or know about which have buttons, and where are they on various garments?

English
● How many different statements can the children think of to say about a particular button? For example, 'My button is blue. I think it was on a party dress.' Try using a button as a fullstop at the end of each sentence.
● Draw a picture of yourself, labelling button fastenings such as: cuffs, shirt fronts, chin straps, epaulettes.
● What happens when buttons fall off, or other clothes need mending? Make a shopping list of items to include in a repair kit (scissors, thread, pins, needle, etc.).
● Encourage the children to make a button collection of their own to use in class. Make up a poster, leaflet, or write a letter home asking for donations.
● Describe how different creatures/people could possibly mistake a button for something else. For example, a bird might imagine it was a juicy snail, or a princess may think she has found her lost jewel.

Maths
● Sort buttons by colours, size or number of holes. Display on a Carroll grid.
● How many buttons can you thread before the timer runs out? Older children could record results for their group.
● Take three buttons and use mirror reflections to 'make' 6,4,2 buttons (or other numbers).
● Start some button sequences for your friend to complete. Think about: number of holes, sizes, shapes.

● **Thread six buttons on a lace.** Separate them to show different ways of making six. Record your findings.

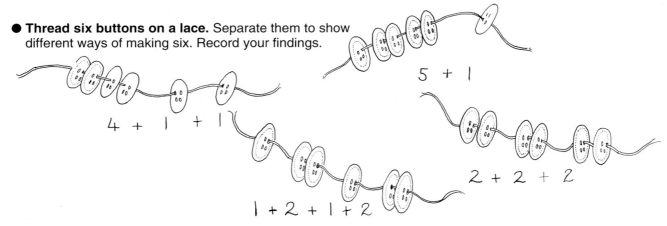

● Do all shirts have seven buttons? Survey and interpret the results - how do you account for the differences?

Science
● Sort buttons by materials (plastic, metal, wood); or properties (opaque, shiny, smooth).
● Which buttons give the clearest rubbings or imprints? Give reasons for your observations.
● What sound does a button make when it's dropped on a table? Try dropping buttons on different surfaces (carpet, tin lid, polystyrene). Which surfaces deaden/amplify sounds?
● Survey the sorts of materials which have buttons as fastenings (fabric, leather, etc.). Can the children think of reasons why they may not be used on stone, wood, paper...?

Art and Craft/Technology
● Use buttons to make jewellery: rings, bracelets, brooch, necklace, etc. (see display photograph).
● Make tangled thread patterns by putting a pencil crayon through a button hole and moving it around the paper in a looped trail. Try using smaller/larger buttons or different colour pencil trails.
● Make a Tiddly Winks game board. Ensure that the scoring spaces and the collection tub are large enough to accommodate the button.
● Find a way of attaching five buttons to a 'shop display card'. Try threading them on wool, string, pipe cleaners; pressing on to sticky tape/Blu Tack, or sewing.

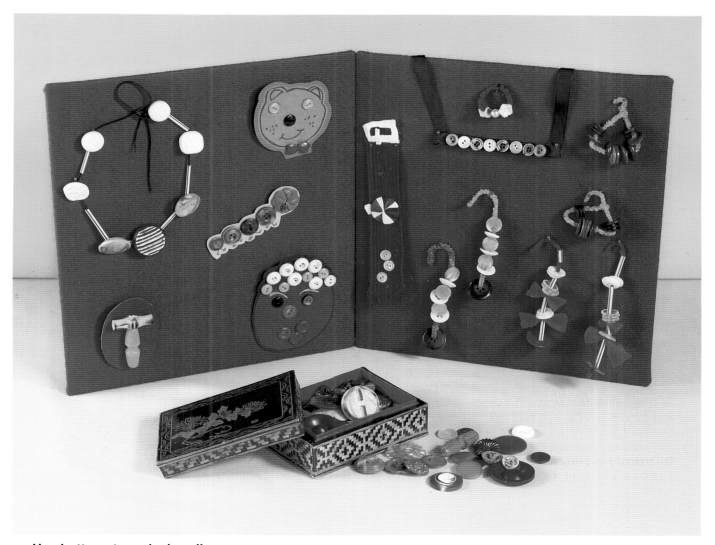

Use buttons to make jewellery

● **Choose three or four buttons to incorporate into a collage** of a clown, train, magic cloak, etc.

Music

● Explore different ways of making sounds with buttons. How will you have to move the buttons to make: a shuffling sound; one short, sharp sound; rattling sounds? Try making buttons sound like raindrops on a window; a giant munching cornflakes; wheels on scrunchy gravel.
● Make simple shakers by putting buttons in lidded pots - how many different ways can these be played - shaking, rolling, swirling movements?

Hall time

● Play Button Chase: divide the children into groups of five, and make one member of each group 'it'. The four other children in each group join hands in a circle round the catcher. The catcher says 'I went to the shops and I bought a ball' (or any other word beginning with B). On hearing 'BUTTONS!' groups drop hands and are chased by their group's 'it'. Whoever is caught first becomes the catcher next time.

Cards

COLLECT: a range of greetings and post cards in a variety of shapes and sizes.

Starters
Show the children your collection and discuss the different sizes, shapes, patterns and greetings. Talk about special occasions when they send and receive cards.

English
● Cut out and discuss some of the phrases used in greetings cards. Play a game of matching the card front to the message inside.
● Choose an interesting card front and use it as part of a story sequence. Draw/describe what might have happened before and after your chosen picture.
● Spy on a card: take a large piece of paper and cut out a 'peep hole'. Move the paper around the card front. What clues can the children spot to guess the picture underneath?
● Choose a celebrations card and make a party invitation or gift tag to complement its theme.
● Turn a greetings card into a postcard. Discuss the postcard format, then divide the reverse side of the picture into two sections. Use to practise writing addresses and holiday greetings.

Maths
● Order the cards by height. Investigate whether the tallest card is also the widest.
● Classify cards by making 'assortment packs', e.g. a set of six - two each of birthday, New Year, and anniversary cards; or, try assortment packs of patterns, animals or flowers.
● Use cards to measure the areas of large surfaces, e.g. tables, P.E. mat, junk box lid.

● **Place six cards side by side - how far do they reach?** Can you make the same six cards cover a shorter/longer distance?

● How many different ways can you find to cut a card in half?
● Can you find a set of cards which tessellate to cover your desk?

Science/Technology
● Choose a small number of cards to recognise by touch alone. Can the children identify: raised borders, holes, badges, holograms, glitter?
● Investigate how a card moves through the air. Compare cards of different sizes and shapes. Can you make the card move in a different way (folding into spinners/aeroplanes, cutting spirals)?
● Make an envelope to fit a chosen card. Ensure that the card can be taken in and out easily.
● Cut a selection of cards in half to make a memory game using the matching pairs.
● Make stick puppets to use in role play. Cut out parts of cards (e.g. teddy's face) and add embellishments.
● Design and make a frame to fit a card. Use techniques which complement your chosen card (see display photograph).

Humanities
● Talk about and label a picture: recognise geographical features such as: trees, buildings, mountain, river, icicles, steep roof.

Design and make a frame to fit a card

● Order and display cards on to an age time-line, e.g. from the arrival of a baby; birthdays; coming of age...to retirement.

● **Look at a picture and make up some symbols** (like a key on a map) to represent elements on the card.

Music
● Make a simple sound sequence to capture the mood and tone of the card's picture, e.g. a winter scene or celebration. Encourage the children to think carefully about which instruments to use for things like: melting icicles (glockenspiel), footsteps in the snow (triangle), popping balloons (woodblocks), unwrapping presents (guiro)...

Hall time
● Have four cards showing, for example, a snowman, clown, bird, car. Allocate each child to one of the cards. Starting from a base line facing you, the children move slowly forward in character (flapping wings, steering, etc.), until you hold up one of the four cards. This is the signal to freeze. Children must return to base if they match to the card shown. Which character reaches you first?

Flowers

COLLECT: an assortment of flowers in a range of colours, sizes, scented/unscented, e.g. poppies, nasturtiums, dog roses, tulips. Seed catalogues and packets.

Starters
Talk about where flowers are found: gardens, parks, garden centres, the school field, florists. Identify similarities and differences between flowers. Use a flip chart to note down the names of flowers the children already know. This could form the beginnings of a flower alphabet. Be sensitive towards hay fever sufferers. Tell the children that parts of flowers may be poisonous - wash hands after handling.

English
● Write a simple description of a flower (colour, shape, number of petals, tall/short...) Can a friend guess which flower you are describing?
● Write a 'thank you' gift tag to accompany a bouquet for a special person in school, e.g. an end of term 'thank you' to a school helper.
● Show what happened the day you found the sprite's magic pollen. Do you sprinkle it on dad's beard, travel to a magical land, or use it to escape from the ogre?
● Look at seed packets for information given in words and pictures. Draw your own seed packet and write important headings such as: flower name, picture of flower, planting time, height.

Maths
● Compare how two kinds of flower are the same/different. Look at features such as: shape, number, colour and size of petals and leaves; hollow/solid stem; scent.

● **Design a flower using fuzzy felt/plane shapes.** List the number/type of shapes used. Older children can make the flower symmetrical or use tessellating shapes.

● Choose a flower and count the number of petals. Chart how many petals would be on 2, 3, 4....flowers.
● Show how twelve flowers can be shared equally between 2 (3,4,6,l2) vases. Try other combinations of flowers and vases.
● Use a mirror to spot any lines of symmetry in a flower - does it make a difference if you also look at the stalk/leaves?

● There are two red, two yellow, two orange flowers in a window box. **Draw/list all the different three-flower posies you can make** (R.R.O; R.O.Y...)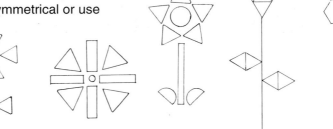

● Look at the information on a seed packet/catalogue. Choose five flowers and chart in order of how tall they are expected to grow.

Science
● Choose a flower and make a close observational drawing. Label parts such as: petal, stem, leaf, seed box, carpel.
● Take one scented flower and devise a fair test to show how far away you can stand and still smell it.
● Investigate how to make scented water. Consider things such as: which parts of the flower to use; should petals be crushed, shredded, dipped in; amount of water (hot or cold).

Use different papers to make concertina cut-out flowers

● Look at the first few pages of a catalogue to investigate which flower colour is the most common. Chart colours found in the pictures or the text. Are there are any colours you cannot find?

Art and Craft/Technology

● Make some florist's wrapping paper - use junk materials to print the flower shapes.

● **Make a vase by decorating a junk pot,** with, for example, cut out flower pictures, collage materials, or by winding thread oddments around it

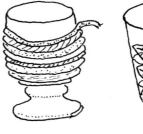

● Create your own imaginary flower, based on observation: it must have petals, a stem, leaves, seed box.
● Make a bouquet of three flowers. How will it be held together (ribbon bow; paper cone; tied with streamers)?

Hall time

● Pot the flower: divide the class into two teams. Give each team the name of a flower beginning with the same letter, e.g. daisy, dahlia. The two teams face each other in lines across the middle of the hall. If you call 'DAHLIA' that team races away from the daisies - who must try to catch them before they reach a home base.

Snails

COLLECT: garden snails in a variety of sizes and colours; an appropriate environment in which to transport them; some empty snail shells.

Starters
Talk to the children about where you found your snails and how you have tried to keep them comfortable. Look carefully at their spiral shaped shells. Brainstorm what the children already know about snails - what else would they like to find out? **Wash hands after handling!**

English
● Think of words describing the snail's appearance and movements (spiral, slide, glide). Display inside a snail shape.
● Make a sequence showing the journey of a snail, e.g. 'I went over the stone, under bushes...'
● Make up a 'How to care for living things' poster.
● Draw and label a picture showing what things might look like to a snail (a puddle is a lake: a pebble is a mountain; a car is a tank).
● Illustrate and caption an occasion when someone might say: 'You're moving at a snail's pace' (e.g. getting ready for bed, clearing up).

Maths
● Roll out two pieces of Plasticine, each 25cm long. Use these to make one large and one smaller spiral. Can you make a clockwise/anti-clockwise spiral?
● Make spiral patterns on peg boards (or squared/dotty paper). Can older children spot a spirals number pattern?
● Use a red crayon to draw a wiggly snail trail across a piece of paper. Draw another trail in a different colour. Estimate, then measure, which is the longest.
● List things you do slowly/carefully (pour a drink; cut out shapes; thread a needle) and those you can do quickly (run, cycle, skip).
● List five comparisons showing the size of a snail shell: 'as big as...a 2p coin/my pencil-sharpener...'

● **Draw some open/closed; curved/angular shapes.** Place them on a grid - where will the spirals fit?

Science
● Make a careful drawing of a snail. Label parts such as: shell, foot, head, breathing hole, tentacles. Older children could describe what it feels/looks like in more detail (shiny, dull, rough).
● Which surfaces will a snail move over? Try: earth, plastic, wood, sandpaper, carpet, polystyrene.
● In which directions can a snail move? Chart how often it moves: forwards, backwards, sideways.
● Have a snail race. How long does it take for them to travel 25cm? Does the largest snail have the biggest foot and travel quicker?
● Look at the trail patterns a snail makes on a piece of dark paper. Label where the path is straight, curved, broken.

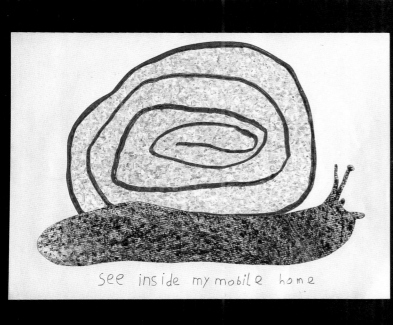

See inside my mobile home

Have a look inside the snail's home

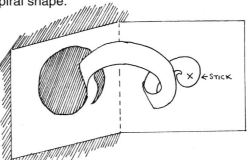

See inside my mobile home

Art and Craft/Technology
- Dribble glue in a winding pattern over the paper. Sprinkle with sand/glitter, to make a snail trail.
- Dip fingers in paint and print by making a snail's rippling foot movements with your hands.
- Make a model of a snail in Plasticine, dough or clay. Create shell textures and patterns with clay tools.
- Make a silhouette picture of a snail in the garden.
- Try making a games board with the number track in a spiral shape.
- **Use a cut-out spiral shape in a snail greetings card.**

Music
- Sing favourite rhymes and songs at normal speed, then have fun changing the tempo - sing them quickly or very slowly.
- Play some snail trails on instruments. Find out how to make a continuous sound on your instrument, e.g. rub the drum rather than tap. Draw a trail on the blackboard with some breaks in the line. Play continuously as someone points along the trail, but be silent in the breaks.

Hall time
- Snail trail game: arrange some barrels, benches, planks and stools as a circuit. Move as snails on tummies/backs round the whole trail.
- Snail races: slide on backs/tummies; roll (lengthwise/curled up) very slowly.

Starting with a Book

LITTLE RED RIDING HOOD
retold by Tony Ross (Picture Puffin)

Starters
How did the children feel towards the characters in the story? Talk about how Red Riding Hood got into danger. What did the wolf do to trick her? Have fun exploring how voices can be disguised. Recall and recount personal 'visiting Grandma' stories.

English
● Make an identity card for Red Riding Hood so Grandma will know who is visiting. Include: eye colour, height, special features (e.g. always wears a red cape).
● Make up a scrumptious menu to cheer up the wolf after his defeat at the cottage.

● **Make a list showing what you would put in a basket** for your Grandma when you visit her next.

● What might Red Riding Hood write in a letter to a friend describing her adventure with the wolf?
● Make a 'How to Keep Safe' leaflet for Grandma. Draw/write some useful reminders: 'Look through the spyhole'; 'Use your door locks and chains'; 'Have a secret knock code'.

Maths
● How many special buns can you make from a piece of Plasticine? Is it possible to make even more? Think about shape, size and thickness of the buns.
● Grandma needs three buttons to finish the cloak. She has green, blue and yellow buttons in her box. How many different three-button combinations could she choose from?
● Take some measurements to help Grandma make you a cape: across the shoulders; around the chest; shoulders to feet; head circumference.
● Red Riding Hood visited Grandma once a week. How many visits could she make this month? What about next/last month? Or in half a term?
● There is a cake and an apple in Red Riding Hood's basket. Chart (over 10-20 tries) which of these the wolf is most likely to take out first. Try adding a biscuit to the basket.

Science and Humanities
● Use magnifiers to explore the 'all the better to see you with' idea. Encourage close observation by drawing pictures before and after magnification of, for example, backs of hands, or a piece of wood.

● **Look at the references to the senses in the wolf's refrain.** Make a senses list of your own, e.g. With my nose I can smell...With my eyes I can see... Older children could map senses used in familiar activities.

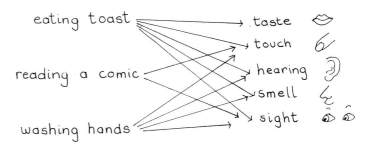

Brainstorm synonyms for the word 'big' and use these to describe the wolf

- Use construction toys, or draw a simple map, showing the woodcutter's house, Grandma's cottage and woodland features. Try directing a friend through Red Riding Hood's journey: along the path, beside the stream, over the stile.
- List the sorts of transport Red Riding Hood might have chosen for her journey to Grandma's. Which ones could cope with bumpy surfaces, narrow lanes, overhanging branches, etc. Which are not practical?

Art and Craft/Technology
- Take rubbings of wood using different coloured crayons. Use the rubbings sheets to cut out shapes for a picture of Grandma's cottage in the wood.
- Use construction toys, or junk, to make a basket big enough to hold two 'cakes'.
- Make yourself a wolf disguise kit, e.g. grandma's glasses, nightcap, false teeth.
- Make a hooded cape to fit a soft toy; or, try making a newspaper cape for a friend.
- Look at what the creatures in the wood are doing (playing football, going out for the evening). Make your own pictures in a similar style, depicting a celebration to mark the Wolf's departure.

Hall time
- Adapt 'What's the Time, Mr Wolf?' by asking: 'What's for dinner, Mr. Wolf?' Everyone's safe on responses such as 'spaghetti' but must run when it's 'RED RIDING HOOD'.
- Play 'Wolf Tag': this time the children are chased as they move around on hands and knees.

MEG'S CAR

H. Nicoll/J. Pienkowski (Picture Puffin)

Starters

Talk to the children about the sorts of journeys we make - which are necessary (home to school/work) and which do we make just for fun? Consider the different types of transport we might use to reach places which are near and far away.

English

● Find and have fun saying the sound words in the book (rattle, bang, tinkle). Add some more of your own and write them in appropriate shapes and lettering.
● Draw the ingredients and/or write a spell to make Meg's car really luxurious.

● **Look at how the words in the story rise as Meg's car starts to fly. Try writing a shape sentence** to describe: a car ride along a winding road; avoiding a pot hole; taking a detour.

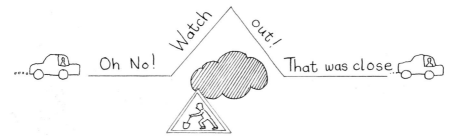

● List all the things you need for a picnic: food and drink; games; towels/flannels; litter bag.

Maths

● Make magical cars using plane shapes. List the number/colour/types of shapes used.
● Collect data on the children's favourite outings. Who has been to the adventure playground, cinema, river, etc?

● **With squared paper/cube board, explore chequered flag patterns** using 4,9,16,25... squares.

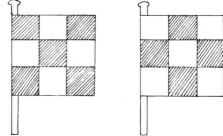

● Choose three figures, for example 1,5,7 - how many different number plates can you make (157, 571, 75l...)? Older children could explore plates using letter/figure configurations.

Science

● Compare how Meg's car might travel over smooth and bumpy surfaces. Use toy cars/Lego models and make ridges and holes using sand, card, Plasticine, stones, bricks.
● Make a Venn diagram comparing what a car needs to keep it running (petrol, oil, water, etc.) with the things we need to keep us going (sleep, food, water...)

● **Devise ways of stopping a car at the bottom of a slope.** Investigate barriers which are soft/hard, tall/low. Try using hands/Plasticine walls, sand or polystyrene mounds.

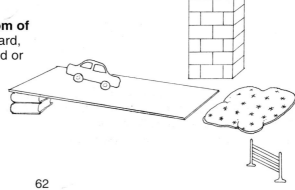

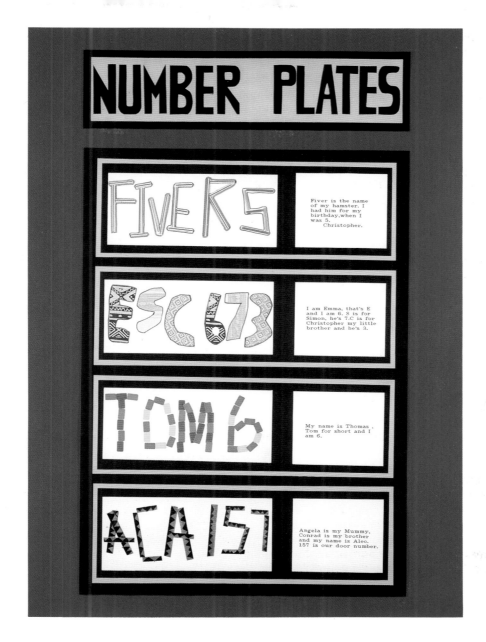

Humanities

● Use farmyard sets or construction toys to make a simple model of the countryside Meg travelled through. Compare her view from the car on the road with what she might see from the 'flying car'.
● Which places have the children visited, or where would they most like to go for an outing? Try recording information such as: is it near or far away? What can you do there? Is it just for children, or would adults like it too?
● Plan and draw a picnic site. Think about: seats, litter bins, parking, toilets, play areas.

Art and Craft/Technology

● Look at Meg's car plate. Make one for yourself using personal letters/numbers (see photograph).
● Design and model a new emblem to replace the witch on the bonnet of Meg's car.
● Look at Meg's 'dream car'. Draw, paint, or use magazine pictures, to create your own crazy, composite vehicles.
● Talk about the silhouette shapes used in the illustrations and make your own pictures in the same style. Try a journey or outing the children have taken, e.g. a coach trip, or a ride on the big dipper.

Hall time

● Play 'Trip Out': children 'drive' around, as if on a journey, listening for you to call out various landmarks (church, bridge, school, garage). They must only stop (to refuel) on the command 'GARAGE'. Try adding more stopping points: cafe, traffic lights etc.
● Litter relay: run relay races with teams picking up four pieces of 'litter' (beanbag, hoop, quoit, ball) on each run.

MRS LATHER'S LAUNDRY
A.Ahlberg/A.Amstutz (Puffin)

Starters
Discuss what the children know about the laundering process. Which facilities do they use at home or in their locality (hand/machine washing, launderette; dry cleaners)? Look at care labels in the children's clothes and talk about what the symbols mean.

English
● Retell the story on seven bubbles showing what happened on each day of the week. Try the same for an alternative family, e.g. Mrs Post gets tired of delivering post cards. What happens on her worst/best day of all?

● **Show the sequence** of Mrs Lather's laundering on cut-out sheet/vest shapes.

● Look at 'pairs' of customers, e.g. the long and short dog. Draw two frames showing opposites such as old/young; tall/short; fat/thin.
● What other names would suit a family of laundry workers? Create and illustrate alliterative names for each member of the family, e.g. Miss Betty Bubble, Master William Washit.
● Draw a picture with a speech bubble of something that drives you crazy.

Maths
● Draw/cut out a set of things that help us wash clothes (bowl, soap powder, scrubbing brush) and a set of things to help wash ourselves (flannel, soap, towel). Are there any overlaps?
● Each child draws a pair of socks. Make a socks number line to practise patterns of 2. If the whole class took their socks to Mrs. Lather, how many would she wash?
● Make a list of the days of the week and help Mrs Lather to plan her work routine, e.g. Monday - washing; Tuesday - drying (then ironing, mending, delivering...)

● **Ask the children to draw all the clothes they are wearing.** Price each item (according to ability). Can they work out how much it costs to launder their clothes?

● Investigate which clothes take up most space in the airing cupboard - shorts, T-shirts, or skirts. Try comparing areas by using real clothing or paper cut-out shapes.

Make some book marks on the story theme

Science
- Can all wet objects be wrung out to dry? Try a sponge, shoe, fabric, paper, etc. Which ones keep their shape? Chart Before and After findings.
- Cut out/draw a set of things which help us do the washing, e.g. soap, bowl, iron, driers. Add captions to show how, for example, the iron's heat helps press clothes, or a peg uses a spring to grip.
- Collect some objects such as: a metal toy, Duplo brick, dolls' clothes, paper. Investigate which of these objects can be cleaned with water. Chart how else we can get things clean - dusting, brushing dried mud, shoe/metal polish.

Technology
- Make some book marks on the story theme (see photograph).
- Make front/top loader washing machines from junk boxes - add dials and a soap dispenser.
- Use Plasticine, dough or junk materials to make Mrs Lather a new soap dish.
- Find ways of attaching cut out/real clothes on to a string washing line. Use combinations of, for example, string, paper clips, pipe cleaners.

Hall time
- Practise 'popping a bubble', e.g. pat-bounce a ball, jump in and out of hoops, throw a beanbag through a hoop target.
- Laundry game: on a start signal, children run around the room listening for movement commands, e.g. 'IRON' means lie flat on the floor, 'BUBBLES' (make a rounded shape), 'DRYING' (spin round on the spot), 'WASHING LINE' (whole class makes a line).

PEACE AT LAST
Jill Murphy (MacMillan)

Starters
Talk about times when, like Mr. Bear, the children have been kept awake at night by noises. Which noises do they like/dislike? Consider other events which may interrupt a good night's sleep (new surroundings, nightmares, etc.). Ask the children to describe their bedtime routines.

English
● Help the children to pinpoint things which kept Mr. Bear awake - can they suggest any others? Try incorporating these into a sequel, keeping the refrain 'I can't stand this!'

● **Make a check list of items** needed in the bedroom and bathroom when getting ready for bed.

● Baby Bear's aeroplane noises irritated Mr. Bear. Can the children illustrate some of their own noisier activities which sometimes annoy others? Show in speech bubbles what people say to you at these times.
● Which favourite stories would the children choose to include in a 'Bedtime Bonanza Book'? Younger children could make a picture contents page. Older children can list contents alphabetically by title/author.

Maths
● Make a simple picture sequence or flow chart of a 'going to bed' routine: tidy up toys, get changed/washed, read story.
● Think about the noises in the book. Sort them into animal sounds and others (machine, people noises). Draw/find pictures of other sound makers to add to these sets.
● Talk about comparative sizes of the Bear family. Try representing them in models using construction toys. Some children could make bears in three specific weights (e.g. 50, 100, 150gm).
● Collect data to find out if the children usually go to bed before or after Baby Bear.

● Get a feel of the length of time that Mr. Bear stayed awake (from 9pm - 7am).
Make a ten-hour time-line showing all the activities the children might have done in that amount of time.

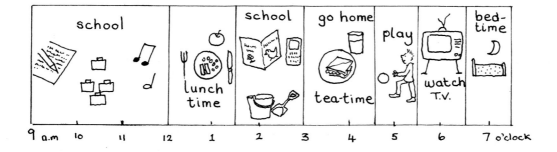

Humanities
● Show on a picture, plan or model, the sequence of places visited by Mr. Bear during his wakeful night. Which rooms were upstairs/downstairs? Which locations were inside/outside?
● Discuss noises associated with different locations (gardens, shops, swimming pool). Draw a busy picture of one of these places, showing as many 'sound makers' as possible. Add the appropriate noises in sound bubbles.

Design a games board based on the story

● Show on a sorting diagram the places in school where we are allowed to be noisy, e.g. the playground, and where we must be quiet (carpet corner, library). In which places is it fine to be noisy sometimes but not at others?

Art and Craft/Technology
● Use junk materials to make a bed just the right size for a Lego person or soft toy.
● Design a sign for Mr. Bear's door requesting peace and quiet, e.g. 'Hush please', 'Bear sleeping'.
● Make a wax and scratch picture of your living room at night showing lights on/off, activities etc.

● **Make a night time mobile using cut out silhouette shapes** of the nocturnal animals shown in the book.

● Look at the illustrations - how does the colour of the sky changes towards dawn? Mix paint shades to create the same effect. Use as a background for a collage of a favourite part of the Mr. Bear story.

Music
● Join in with the story: divide the children into two groups - one to make appropriate sounds for the noise words, the other to chant the refrain 'I can't stand this'. Extend to instruments: one group taps out the rhythm of the refrain (on tambour/drum), and the other group selects instruments to evoke, for example, the ticking clock (wood blocks); the leaking tap (triangle).

Hall time
● Play 'Match up': divide the class into four groups. Have two action groups (one to be the clock, one to represent birds) and two 'sound' groups ('tick-tock' and 'tweet-tweet'). The action groups move around while miming bird and clock movements, while the sound groups make their given noises. The aim is for the children to find their appropriate pair - a clock matches up to tick-tock.

THE VERY BUSY SPIDER
Eric Carle (Hamish Hamilton)

Starters
What do the children already know about farms and farming jobs? Discuss the animals in the story focusing on size, what they look and sound like, and what they eat. Where have the children seen spiders/webs - what are they for, and how does the spider make them?

English
● Make up a poem based on the animal sounds in the book and other farmyard noises. End each four-line verse with 'What a noise!'
● 'The spider didn't answer', but what might it be thinking? Put ideas into thought bubbles, e.g. 'My legs are killing me'; 'Nearly finished'; 'Time for dinner'.

● **Make word webs of, for example,** busy words; touch words; words to describe the different ways things are said (grunted, squeaked, barked).

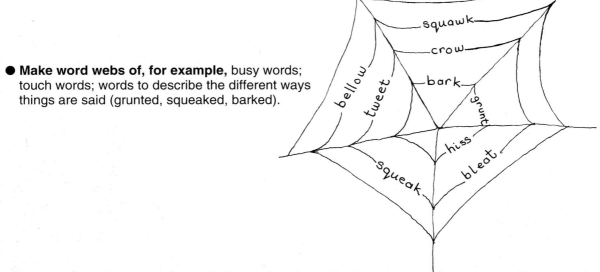

● Make a simple sequel to the book. Try putting the spider in a pet shop, forest or seaside - what do different animals say to the spider now?

Maths
● Make a web shape with six geo-strips (or strips of paper). Spot and chart how many 3/4/5...sided shapes there are inside the web.
● Using the animals in the book, find different ways of making a total of eight legs, e.g. I fly + I duck; 2 cows. Try other totals. Can there ever be an odd number total?
● Investigate different ways of making spirals: drawing and cutting from plain/squared paper; peg board; cube tray. Can the children spot any number patterns?
● The spider's web grew - investigate ways of making numbers grow, e.g. repeated addition; doubling; using the constant facility on a calculator; triangular/square numbers.

Science/Humanities
● How many legs has a spider? Do the children know any creatures with more/fewer legs? Make a table showing animals with 0,2,4,6,8, more than 8, legs.
● Draw and match farm animals to their special housing: the horse lives in the stable; pig in the sty...
● Use construction/junk materials to make a farm layout. Write labels showing: barns, fields, machines, pond, farmhouse...
● Compare and contrast two of the animals in the story, e.g. the cat and duck. Record information about size, number of legs, type of coat or feet.

Art and Craft/Technology
● Look at the raised autograph in the book. Make your own initials using: wool, sand on glue, straws.

- Make some spiders. Use stuffed paper circles or yoghurt pots for the body, and embellish with collage materials (see photograph).
- Paint your own version of a spectacular sun like the one in the story. Mix shades of yellow and red on a piece of paper, cut out and arrange in sun ray shapes.

- **Make a simple card 'pairs' game** matching the animals in the book to their sounds.

- Design some spider webs. Try: weaving coloured threads around straws or through fruit nets; cutting 'snowflake' patterns, sprinkling glue trails with salt (see display photograph).

Music
- Play a guiro/cabasa to represent the sounds of the farmer on his tractor. Add to this tractor refrain the sounds heard in the different farm areas visited, and the jobs done, e.g. the grunts and squeals of the pigs feeding, rounding up the sheep, brushing the yard, collecting eggs.

Hall time
- Play 'Trapped flies': choose four children to be 'flies' and divide the rest of the class into groups of four as 'spiders' webs'. The webs join hands and chase the flies, trying to trap them in a circle. The first group to catch a fly in their 'web' become the next flies to be chased.

69

Five minute fillers

Circle stories: you start, then the children take turns around a circle to contribute to a story. Try incorporating some real objects (e.g. soft toy, shoe, feather) from time to time.

Deliberate mistakes: revisit favourite nursery rhymes or action songs (see Resources, page 71). Make some deliberate mistakes for the children to spot.

Hangman: adapt the traditional game by focusing on word endings ('ng', 'ed', the 'magic e'). Try other letter strings.

Pondering on pictures: consider the illustrations in two different picture books. How are they the same and different? What tools and techniques have the artists used? Encourage the children to share what they like or dislike about the illustrations.

Number solvers: can the children discover which number you are thinking about by asking questions such as: is it more/less than 10? How many digits? Odd or even?

Beep: take turns to count in order round a circle. Substitute the word BEEP for every third number (1, 2 beep etc.). Try beep for odd/even numbers, or any number with a 2 in it (2, 12, 20...).

Number change: on separate pieces of paper, write three figures, e.g. 1, 7, 8. Give these to the children to hold. How can they position themselves to make different three digit numbers?

Kim's game: this time, arrange the objects in rows/columns. Can the children name the missing object and tell you which position it was in? Or, try working out which two objects have changed places.

Hunt the shape: how many circles (squares, oblongs) can the children spot from where they are? Which shape can they see most of?

Follow me: establish a steady body sound pattern (e.g. foot stamps). Children join in, ready to change the sounds as soon as they spot you change from stamps to claps (mouth pops, chest slaps...)

Rhythm riddles: clap the rhythm of a favourite song or rhyme: can the children guess which one it is? Can they clap some themselves for others to guess?

Make connections: compare any two objects; discuss how many things they have in common - colour, texture, natural/man-made...

Odd one out: name items belonging to a chosen category (animals, food, transport). Can the children recognise the odd one out?

I Spy materials: give the traditional game of 'I spy' a materials focus, e.g. 'I spy something made of paper (wood, metal); it is used for...'

Stop, listen and identify the sounds around you. Are they near or far away? Can the children sort them into: sounds made by people/machines?

Guessing jobs: mime actions associated with different jobs (cook, racing driver, plumber). Can others guess what you do?

Resources

Anthologies for:
Stories
A treasury of stories from around the world, chosen by L. Jennings (Kingfisher). *Fairy tales,* T. Jones (Puffin). *Fairy tale treasury,* selected by V. Haviland (Hamish Hamilton). *Meet my friends,* chosen by K. Webb (Puffin). *Stories f or (6, 7, 8) year olde.* S & S Corrin (Puffin). *Ten in a bed,* A.Ahlberg/A.Amstutz (Puffin). *The Kingfisher treasury of stories for children,* N & E Blishen (Kingfisher). *The Puffin children's treasury,* selected by C.Fadiman (Viking Kestrel). *Time for Telling,* selected by M.Medlicott (Kingfisher).

Music
Silly Aunt Sally, J. Holdstock (Ward Lock Educational) *The music box songbook* (BBC). A & C Black books: *Apusskidu; Birds and Beasts; Count me in; Harlequin; Mango spice; Okki-tokki-unga; Tinder-box.*

Finger/Action/Nursery Rhymes
Over the moon (Walker). *The Kingfisher playtime treasury,* selected by P. Corbett (Kingfisher). *The Mother Goose treasury,* R. Briggs (Puffin). *This Little Puffin,* compiled by E. Matterson (Puffin).

Poetry
A pot of gold, compiled by J. Bennett (Corgi) *A very first/Another very first/A first poetry book,* compiled by J. Foster (OUP) *First poems,* compiled by J. Eccleshare (Orchard Books). *Madtail, miniwhale,* chosen by W. Magee (Puffin). *Poems for the very young,* selected by M. Rosen (Kingfisher). *Poetry corner,* ed. C. Smith (BBC). *Say it again granny!* J. Agard (Little Mammoth). *Scholastic Collections - Poetry:* compiled by W. Magee (Scholastic). *The Puffin book of 20th century children's verse,* ed. B. Patten (Puffin). *The Walker book of poetry for children,* compiled by J. Prelutsky (Walker).

RESOURCES RELATING TO TOPICS THROUGHOUT THE BOOK

ALPHABET: Book: *Amazing Alphabets,* L.Bruce (Frances Lincoln). *Mog's Amazing Birthday Caper,* J.Kerr (Picture Lions). **Poetry:** 'An alphabet of questions', C.E. Carryl, in *A pot of gold* (Corgi).

BOXES AND BOTTLES: Book: *Dear Zoo,* R.Campbell (Picture Puffin). *The gift,* J.Prater (Picture Puffin). **Poetry**: 'In this box', J. Fairfax in *Madtail, Miniwhale,* chosen by W.Magee (Puffin). **Music:** 'Ten green bottles', in *This Little Puffin,* compiled by E.Matterson (Puffin).

CHANGES: Book: *Changes, Changes,* P.Hutchins (Bodley Head). *The Hungry Caterpillar,* E. Carle. **Poetry:** *Hairy Tales and Nursery Crimes,* M.Rosen (Fontana). **Music:** 'It happens each spring', in *Harlequin* (A&C Black).

COLOUR: Book: *Elmer,* D.McKee (Red Fox). *The mixed-up chameleon,* E.Carle (Picture Puffin). **Poetry:** *Colours,* S. Hughes (Walker). **Music:** 'Sing a rainbow', in *Apusskidu* (A&C Black).

DOORS AND WINDOWS: Book: *Is anyone home?* R.Maris (Puffin). **Poetry:** 'The Window Cleaner', M.Long, in *Poems for the very young,* selected by M.Rosen (Kingfisher).

GET THE MESSAGE: Book: *Shy Charles,* R.Wells (Picture Lions). **Poetry:** 'Going through the old photos', M.Rosen in *A first poetry book,* compiled by J.Foster (OUP). Music: Talkin in *Tinderbox,*(A & C Black).

HANDS AND FEET: Book: *The mice who lived in a shoe,* R.Peppe (Puffin). **Poetry:** 'Tiptoe', K.Kuskin, in *A pot of gold,* compiled by J.Bennett (Corgi). **Music:** 'Kaigal-Hands' in *Tinder-box* (A & C Black).

HOLES: Book: *Holes and Peeks,* A.Jonas (Walker). **Poetry:** 'Rosemary's teeth', M. Dugan in *A first poetry book,* compiled by J.Foster (OUP). **Music:** 'There's a hole in my bucket', in *Apusskidu* (A&C Black).

LINES: Book: *Mrs Mopple's washing line,* A.Hewett (Picture Puffin). **Poetry:** 'Telephone wires', J. Brown in *Madtail, Miniwhale,* chosen by W.Magee (Puffin). **Music:** 'A Fishy Tale', in *Silly Aunt Sally* (Ward Lock).

MARKING TIME: Book: *The stopwatch,* D.Lloyd/P.Dale (Walker). **Poetry:** 'In one second', I.Souter, in *Scholastic Collections: Poetry,* compiled by W.Magee (Scholastic). **Music:** 'Song of the clock' in *Tinderbox,* (A&C Black).

MONSTERS: Book: *The very worst monster,* P.Hutchins (Puffin). **Poetry** 'The Bogus-boo', J. Reeves in *A first poetry book,* compiled by J.Foster (OUP). **Music:** 'It's a monster', D. Moses in *Scholastic Collections: Songs,* compiled by P.Morrell.

MOVING ABOUT: Book: *I wish I could fly,* R.Maris (Picture Puffin). **Music:** *Okki-Tokki-unga, a book of action songs* (A&C Black).

NEWSPAPER: Book: *The true story of the three little pigs,* J.Scieszka (Picture Puffin).

NUMBERS ALL AROUND: Book: *Millions of cats,* W.Gag (Puffin). **Poetry:** 'I'm only a number 2', S.Stewart, in *Madtail, Miniwhale,* chosen by W.Magee (Puffin). **Music:** *Count me in* (songs about numbers, A&C Black).

OLD MOTHER HUBBARD: Book: *Old Mother Hubbard*, C.Hawkins (Little Mammoth). *Rhyme in The Mother Goose Treasury*, R.Briggs (Puffin). **Music:** 'Old Mother Hubbard', in *Sing hey diddle diddle* (A&C Black).

OPPOSITES: Book: *Lost and found*, J. Mogensen (Hamish Hamilton). **Poetry:** 'As wet as a fish', in *First Poems*, compiled by J.Ecleshare (Orchard Books). **Music:** 'Up and down', in *Silly Aunt Sally* (Ward Lock).

OUR SCHOOL: *Starting School*, J.A. Ahlberg (Picture Puffin). **Poetry:** School poems in *Another First Poetry Book*, compiled by J.Foster (OUP).

PUZZLE IT OUT: Book: *If at first you do not see*, R.Brown (Red Fox). **Poetry:** 'Who?' J.Catermull in *A first poetry book*, compiled by J.Foster (OUP). **Music:** 'Can anyone tell me that?' in *Tinder-box*.

RAINY DAYS: Book: *Bringing the rain to Kapiti Plain*, V.Aardema (PictureMac). **Poetry:** Selection in *Poems for the very young* (Kingfisher). **Music:** 'The rain song', in *Harlequin*, (A&C Black).

STRING AND THINGS: Book: *Tom's rainbow walk*, C.Anholt (Little Mammoth). **Poetry:** *The Kingfisher Playtime Treasury*, selected by P.Corbett. **Music:** 'Kite Song' in *Silly Aunt Sally* (Ward Lock).

TAKE SIX: *Six dinner Sid*, I.Moore (Simon & Schuster). **Music:** *Count me in, songs and rhymes about numbers* (A&C Black).

THE THREE BILLY GOATS GRUFF: Book: *The Three Billy Goats Gruff*, J.Langley (Picture Lions).

AUTUMN SEEDS AND LEAVES: Book: *Conker*, Stopwatch books, A &C Black. **Music:** 'Let's collect conkers', in *Harlequin* (A&C Black).

BUTTONS: Book: 'The lost button' in *Frog and toad are friends*, A.Lobel. **Poetry:** 'Buttons' by W.Kingdom-Ward in *Poems for the very young*, (Kingfisher).

CARDS: Book: *The Jolly Postman*, J.& A.Ahlberg (Heinemann). **Poetry:** 'Happy birthday Dilroy!' in *I din do nuttin*, J. Agard (Little Mammoth).

FLOWERS: Book: *What's inside? Plants* (Dorling Kindersley). **Poetry:** 'Learning the flowers', E. Finney, in *Scholastic Collections: Poetry*, compiled by W.Magee.

SNAILS: Book: *Snail*, Stopwatch books (A & C Black). **Poetry:** 'Snail', J. Drinkwater in *First Poems*, compiled by J.Eccleshare (Orchard Books). **Music:** 'Melancholy snail', in *Silly Aunt Sally* (Ward Lock).

LITTLE RED RIDING HOOD: Books: *Little Red Riding Hood*, J. Langley (Picture Lions). and *Look out, he's behind you*, T.Bradman/M.Chamberlain (Little Mammoth).

MEG'S CAR: Books: *Mr. Gumpy's motor car*, J.Burningham. **Poetry:** 'The car trip', M.Rosen in *A pot of gold*, compiled by J.Bennett (Corgi). **Music:** 'Getting about songs', in *The Music Box Songbook* (BBC).

MRS LATHER'S LAUNDRY: Book: *The Wild Washerwomen*, J.Yeoman/Q.Blake (Picture Puffin). **Poetry:** 'Launderama', I.C.Smith in *A very first poetry book*, compiled by J.Foster (OUP).

PEACE AT LAST: Book: *Goodnight Owl!* P.Hutchins (Picture Puffin). **Poetry:** *Noisy Poems*, collected by J.Bennett (OUP).

THE VERY BUSY SPIDER: Book: *Emily's legs*, D.K.Smith (Macdonald). **Poetry:** 'The Spider's web', M.Holmes in *Madtail, Miniwhale* (Puffin). **Music:** 'Buttercup farm' in *Silly Aunt Sally* (Ward Lock).

For details of further Belair Publications please write to:
BELAIR PUBLICATIONS LTD.
P.O. Box 12, Twickenham TW1 2QL, England.

For sales and distribution (outside USA and Canada):
Folens Publishers, Albert House, Apex Business Centre,
Boscombe Road, Dunstable, Beds. LU5 4RL, England.

For sales and distribution in USA and Canada:
Belair Publications USA, 116 Corporation Way, Venice, Florida, 34292.